LD

D1484778

GETTING STAFF EXCITED

THE ROLE OF THE

NURSE MANAGER

(AND OTHERS TOO)

IN LONG TERM CARE

BY LEN FABIANO

SECOND EDITION

P ·R ·E · S· S

FCS International provide a wide range of services to the health care industry including; in-house seminars, publications and audio-visual material.

For further information and a free catalogue, contact:

FCS International
(800)387-8143
Web Site: www.fabconinc.com

DEDICATED TO:

Ron Martyn, friend and associate, whose knowledge and skills have been of significant value to me.

There are few who cross our paths
with the ability to challenge and teach us,
making what we do rewarding and exciting.

Len

Acknowledgments

To all the staff and managers who have helped me to understand the challenges and rewards of the job we do.

To Cheryl Graham who has become a valuable asset to my work and our organization. To Robbie Sprules, your creativity and contributions have been impressive and highly valued.

To my family - my wife Linda, my son Daniel and my daughter Kimberly - for their patience and help, for their understanding and love. A special thanks to Daniel (at age 11) for drawing the picture of the wheelbarrow and managers. Even though you have grown, I will not change it.

Len

ABOUT THE AUTHOR

MR. LEN FABIANO, is a long time practitioner in the aging field, working with both seniors and their families. He has over 28 years experience as a gerontologic counselor and educator. Currently, he serves as a consultant and trainer to long term care facilities and organizations. Mr. Fabiano enjoys respect and recognition as a leader in the care and services for the elderly, and in particular, those suffering from Alzheimer's and other dementias. Over 220,000 individuals have attended Len Fabiano seminars, in excess of 40,000 of Len Fabiano's best selling texts have been sold, and hundreds of facilities and organizations have sought his expertise to assist them in enhancing their efficiency and care.

Mr. Fabiano is the founder and CEO of FCS International. FCS has become a well recognized and dynamic corporation specializing in education and consulting services to health care organizations (with a focus on long term care). FCS publishes and distributes Mr. Fabiano's books worldwide, and produces his popular seminar series. FCS provides consulting services to help organizations improve staff/management relations and overall efficiency, and enhance direct care programs and environmental design.

CONTENTS

	YOU MUST BEGIN HERE	i
CHAPTER 1	IN THE BEGINNING	1
CHAPTER 2	WHERE'S THE PROBLEM	11
CHAPTER 3	LONG TERM CARE	40
CHAPTER 4	STAFFING DYNAMICS	68
CHAPTER 5	ORGANIZATIONAL DYNAMICS	90
CHAPTER 6	ON BECOMING AN EFFECTIVE MANAGER	118
CHAPTER 7	DEALING WITH TODAY'S ISSUES	156
CHAPTER 8	CREATING THE UPWARD SPIRAL	176
CHAPTER 9	RECOGNITION	201
CHAPTER 10	THE FINAL CURTAIN	218
	BIBLIOGRAPHY	228
	INDEX	232

YOU MUST BEGIN HERE

As a manager your job is to get staff. Either get them excited or get them fired. You cannot afford anything in-between. As we will demonstrate, getting staff fired is not only counter-productive, but an admission that a manager has not effectively done his/her job. The effective manager strives to get staff excited about what they do and where they do it.

The first edition of this text called <u>The Nurse Manager (& Others Too) in Long Term Care</u> has been highly successful, but it needed to be revised. Initially the first edition was intended primarily for managers. I soon discovered that it was also purchased by many staff as well. They were excited about its content. Many shared with me that the book allowed them to understand the pressures they and their managers experienced and some of the strategies they could implant to resolve them. It was pleasing to prove that getting staff excited was to get them involved and productive - the only way to achieve quality.

As with any such work, the content and concepts presented in the first edition have evolved and expanded since their inception. My consultations with scores of facilities and organizations over the years and my contact with thousands of managers and staff who have attended my seminars always emphasized one simple fact outlined in that first book - *a strong, positive relationship between staff and managers within any organization allows them to achieve effectiveness and efficiency.* To gain that strong relationship, the people working in that setting must become excited about where they work and what they do. It is time that the cornerstone of that first edition be expanded to the next level. The basic concept that threaded throughout that text stated - *the level of care provided by staff is totally reflective of how well the facility takes care of its staff.*

Long term care is in a time of flux. Financial resources are tight; the philosophy of long term care has evolved to include more sophisticated concepts than existed in the past; our clientele is older and more complex; the demands on staff have increased; and the scrutiny by the community has intensified. All of these have placed considerable demands on the care team to be more efficient and effective. The success of the team is based on the skills of the leader. The leader is the manager. If the manager is effective, then the team is effective. If the manager is ineffective, then the team will be ineffective.

This introduces an important characteristic of management - *the reputation of the organization is not based on what the manager does, but what the manager allows his/her staff to do.* Regardless of the sophistication and progressiveness of the programming within an organization, it is the staff within that facility who will bring the desired reputation to fruition. This can be demonstrated with a simple example. When a family member is upset because her mother is crying over an incident, what will that family member remember? That the facility has an attractive enclosed courtyard for its wanderers or that a staff member has taken five minutes to calm the family member down and resolve mother's problem. Programming, the *things* within the facility will enhance its reputation. But it is the **people**, not the *things* that define its reputation. The actions or inactions of staff will have the greatest impact on family and reflect how the community perceives the facility. The reputation of how caring the facility is really reflects how caring the staff are. Investing in the "things" will have its benefits, investing in the **people** who use the things will create the desired results.

This emphasizes the uniqueness of long term care. The nurse manager within *do not* and *cannot* manage as other industries may. We do not have the manpower, time or resources to have managers consistently monitor staff's performance and check the quality of their work. The majority of managers in long term care are *working managers*. As will be demonstrated in later chapters, the nurse manager in long term care does more than just supervise staff.

Even if the opportunity were available, it is still not possible. There can be six staff on duty caring for forty-two residents during one shift. When the nurse manager is in the room monitoring the care of one staff member, the others are elsewhere performing their job without supervision.

Success within our organization can only be achieved when staff are *self-managed*. This concept will appear frequently throughout this text. When staff are *self-managed*, they are motivated to think, to determine for themselves what is best for their client, or the job to be performed, and to do it to the best of their ability. Many will ask how this can be achieved. The reality is that in many facilities it already exists. In others it is a long way off.

To understand what creates a strong staff/management relationship and a self-managed, excited staff, let us examine a similar relationship - marriage. The relationship dynamics occurring within a marriage are similar to those within an organization. Relationships are relationships whether it involves two people or two hundred people.

Imagine that you and I are married. We view our marriage as a partnership. We talk with each other about everything and anything. This conversational pattern not only centers around the things that bother us, but also on those things that are important to us, the things we enjoy and those we strive for. This ongoing communication cannot be trivialized. In a relationship, the more the partners talk with each other the more they understand each other's perceptions, needs, aspirations, fears and values. Over time I will know more and more how you see things and how you respond to them. This insight into the other's world ensures understanding. In fact when a married couple maintains ongoing communication, they soon find less of a need to talk about such issues. It is not uncommon in a long-standing positive marriage for one partner to say something and the other to respond "I was just thinking about that."

Constant communication ensures effective problem solving. In such a marriage there are few surprises. The more we discuss, the more we uncover and raise issues before they become serious concerns. This means that we will generally deal with each concern at the appropriate time, utilizing each other's abilities to resolve things as they arise.

A strong marriage relationship has one other valuable component - ongoing expression of affection towards each other. Some will say "That is nice!" They have missed the point. To express affection is to tell the other person how much that person is respected and what that person means to the other.

With these dynamics in place, we will undoubtedly develop a strong, close relationship - one that maintains ongoing communication, effective problem solving and consistent expression of affection.

Imagine that after 24 years of such a marriage, I am laid off from my job. How are we? I don't mean our financial state, but our relationship. Will we allow the fact that I am laid off to destroy our twenty four year marriage? Unlikely! In fact it may even draw us closer together. For some that is hard to believe. If you understand the dynamics of a strong relationship, you will understand what occurs. After twenty four years we have become sensitive to each other. You know that I am frustrated because I am unable to find a job. I know that you are pressured because we are unable to make ends meet without my contribution. We will work this out and probably become even stronger as a result of it.

Let us bring in the other players in the relationship - our children. In this marriage, it is unlikely that we will take out our frustrations of my being laid off out on our children. Agreed, our children will not have the *things* that they are accustomed to, but our family unit will remain intact. Ours is a relationship that is built on many strengths. We will not allow it to dissolve because one part of it has been challenged. It is the strength of our relationship that will allow us to resolve the problems encountered. It is the excitement that exists within that relationship that we will tap to allow us to meet the challenges we now face.

Change the scenario. Imagine again that you and I are married. This time the situation is very different. We do not nurture the relationship to ensure that it grows and strengthens. Instead we take that relationship for granted, believing that it will develop on its own as time passes. The skills of communication, problem solving and expressing affection are neglected. We never talk with each more than what is necessary. Even though we are married, we live very separate lives, developing minimal if any closeness. Limited conversation means that we probably do not understand each other well. Without "talking together," we are unable to share perceptions, values, needs, aspirations, etc. Poorly understanding each other restricts our ability to understand how and why the other responds to the things encountered.

Our not "talking" results in problems, issues and concerns just surfacing. When this occurs, there exists an urgency to have them resolved. The difficulty is that these can only be resolved by "talking them out". Our lack of experience in talking with each other, combined with our lack of understanding of the other's perceptions, creates a potential for conflict. This conflict occurs when we are confronted with the same problem, but appear to look at it from opposing sides. Without knowing how the other person sees the situation, it is impossible to relate to what that person is focusing on. This creates a win/lose situation. The more I believe that you do not see it as I do, the more I become frustrated when you do not agree with me. The more you believe that my point of view is all that is emphasized, the more you feel misunderstood, raising your frustrations. The discussion soon turns into an argument.

When either of us feels that we are losing the argument, our emotions seem to dominate. If being logical cannot sway you to "my side," then the only alternative is to intimidate you into submission by raising my voice. As I raise my voice, you will raise yours in retaliation. Emotions soon become the driving force. At some point this loss of control will result in one of us saying something that is not meant. It just seems to "come out wrong." The other person will be hurt by the comment. It is then necessary for that person to retaliate. This confrontational posturing will continue until one or both parties shut down or walk out in frustration. Nothing is resolved except to create negative feelings about the other and our relationship as a whole. Each time an altercation such as this occurs, we become even more reluctant to talk to the other over even the smallest issue for fear of initiating another "blow up."

In this marriage, openly expressing affection towards each other is a rare occurrence. This means that we do not know what we think of each other or how much or even if we respect each other. After twenty four years of such a relationship, communication, problem solving and expressing affection are non-existent. I am then laid off. What happens to our relationship? What impact will it have on our children?

Marriage is an accumulation of positives and negatives. In the first marriage there was a conscious and joint effort to strengthen the relationship by building positives through constant communication, effective problem solving and expressing affection towards each other. These positives are valuable, because they can be cashed in when the going gets rough.

As an example. Every relationship experiences something negative. That negative can be serious enough to result in our not talking to each other for awhile. If the marriage has built and accumulated forty positives, in a short time those positives will outweigh that serious negative. We know how we feel about each other. We know how valuable our partnership is. We will come around and resolve it. The relationship will return to what existed before that negative occurred. In this relationship the couple sees themselves as partners. The strength and skills of one combined with the other allows them to be successful in nearly everything that they encounter. The excitement within this marriage means that each partner sees the other as a valuable asset in making the relationship work.

On the contrary, what would be the impact of accumulating negatives and building few positives? What would *one more* negative do to a relationship that has already accumulated forty negatives and few positives? Endurance and tolerance in dealing with the *forty first* negative would be much less than it was with the eleventh negative. In fact, what becomes the forty first negative could be something very trivial. However, its impact and outcome in a strained marriage would likely have deadly consequences for the relationship. As negatives accumulate, the arguments or blow ups become more frequent. The relationship will inevitably weaken over time and the partnership will likely dissolve.

The two scenarios described above are not unlike organizational relationships.

Like the first marriage discussed, an organization that has strong staff/management relations, excites its people. In this setting there is a belief that a partnership exists between its staff and managers. When staff and managers see themselves as partners, they set very specific expectations of what is needed to fulfill that role. They consciously build thorough and ongoing communication strategies to allow them to work effectively together. This communication pattern establishes a solid foundation to the relationship. It provides an opportunity for each to discover what the other team members value and how they perceive any given situation.

When management/staff relationships are strong, they actively involve both partners in problem solving any and all issues that arise. They know that by combining their efforts, skills and strengths, they will successfully resolve most "things" objectively and thoroughly.

In such a partnership, its members value the efforts of those around them. They intuitively know the importance of ensuring persistent recognition for contributions and achievements. This investing in others adds a unique dimension to the relationship. It demonstrates to all team members that they are respected and valuable, regardless of the job they perform. There is no doubt that the people in this setting will be excited about where they work and what they do. They will believe that it is because of the others and their combined efforts that things are done well. This organization will achieve its goal of quality of life for the residents who live there and quality of work life for those who work there.

Like the second marriage, we can now examine a contrasting organizational scenario. When an organization does not build the relationship between management and staff through effective communication, problem solving and recognition strategies, then the outcome will be very different. The members of this relationship hold a very distinct view - it is "us" and "them", management versus staff, staff versus management. Without ongoing communication, there can be minimal understanding of what the *other* sees, what the *other* believes is important and what the *other* feels is needed to do the job well. In this environment, lack of understanding means a lack of trust and confidence in the *other's* ability. This lack of understanding contaminates any problem solving. Managers will feel that "things" are best handled unilaterally. Their lack of trust in their staff will result in a belief that the safest and easiest course of action in any situation is to dictate to staff what is to be done. They see no need to involve their staff in the problem solving process. This confrontational approach only results in resistance by staff and failure in any attempts to change existing situations. It reinforces a belief by staff that managers do not understand, that *they* cannot be trusted, that *they* do not care.

Recognition in such an organization is usually seen as insignificant and fruitless given the suspicions and distrust that exists. When recognition is lacking, staff and managers alike will neither feel respected nor valuable. When situations sour, there will be an attempt to always blame the other for its downfall. In such a relationship, managers and staff are always critical of any action taken by the *other*, feeling constricted - believing that if it weren't for the *other*, things could be much better. The end result is that quality care will deteriorate, with the residents suffering the brunt of poor moral, inefficiencies and distrust.

What type of relationship does your organization possess?

Let me introduce you to some unique math "$1 + 1 = 1$." What this implies is that staff plus managers equals an effective team. If communication is ongoing, problem solving effective and recognition persistent, then the relationship between the two will be productive and strong and its members excited.

As you will discover, in a relationship where the partners are lacking in the skills and supports to do their job well, where they are not motivated to work to their potential, where they are not encouraged to demonstrate their creativity, the equation changes to "$.89 + .82 = ?$" In reality, the craziness or creativity within an organization is based on the craziness or creativity of the managers and staff within that organization.

Like marriage, organizations are an accumulation of positives and negatives. If managers and staff do not consciously build positives, they will have problems coping with the *difficult times*. To learn how to escape from the dynamics of a negative relationship or how to strengthen positive management/staff relationships, you will want to read on.

This text will show you how *to excite* those around you about what they do and where they do it. More importantly, it will *excite* you to achieve it.

Chapter One

IN THE BEGINNING

There is no better way to know the characters of a play than to stand in the middle of the stage. In order to set the tone for the upcoming chapters, it is important to personalize your experiences as a manager. Answer the following two questions. Until this task is done, the following pages will lack the dimension necessary to make them of value to you.

Take your time and give considerable thought to your answers. Either jot down some notes in the space provided or after each question *raise your eyes* from the page to formulate the answers in your mind:

What have you <u>disliked</u> about the people who have managed you?

What impact did that person(s) have on:
       your enthusiasm?
       your creativity?
       your evaluation of your own work performance and its
          importance?

Undoubtedly, the manager(s) pictured still elicits in you a familiar response. Just thinking about that person probably results in a grimace or a frown as you are reminded of the many frustrations you experienced while working in that environment. Likewise, you most likely detected some physical tension as you recalled the conflicts you encountered. In fact the memory of that manager probably still stirs in you some of the negativity that the relationship created, permanently etching the experience in your mind. It is obvious to you that this type of manager and that person's management style stifled creativity and enthusiasm. Over time it is possible that such a manager caused some staff to dislike their job and where they worked, and to devalue their accomplishments. It is amazing the ability a manager has to paralyze others to the point of apathy. What is your response to the next questions:

What is it that you liked about the manager(s) who motivated you?

What impact did that person(s) have on:
   your enthusiasm?
   your creativity?
   your evaluation of your own work performance and its
      importance?

This manager(s) elicits a very different response. More than likely, thinking about that person causes you to smile as you recall the many wins experienced in that work environment. You probably still feel a twinge of excitement as you are reminded of the many accomplishments while under that person's direction. In fact the memory of that manager probably still stirs in you some of the positive feelings that relationship created, permanently etching the experience in your mind. It is obvious to you that this type of manager, and that person's management style heightened creativity and enthusiasm. Over time those working with this manager not only liked their job, and where they worked, but valued their accomplishments. It is amazing the ability a manager has to excite others to do the best they can.

Managers can be powerful people. This *power* is different than what one would normally think. Often the words "managerial power" conjures up an image of something that can be wielded about in order to get one's way - a belief that when a command is given it will be followed without question. The positive power of management is the ability to mold and influence people - their views of themselves, their job and their workplace. The manager has the ability to excite people to do the best job possible or to deflate them to do only what is necessary, and in some cases as little as possible.

This text demonstrates that power. It shows how to motivate and excite. How to be respected as a leader not a commander. You cannot shun away from your role - you will influence your staff one way or the other. Whether it is the people who manage us or those who we manage, it is the individual who can make the job of managing effective or ineffective.

EXPLAINING THE TITLE

The title <u>Getting Staff Excited: The Role of The Nurse Manager (& Others Too) in Long Term Care</u> raises some immediate question -

What is meant by "Getting Staff Excited"?
Why discuss only long term care?

To the question about *getting staff excited*. Ours is a business where quality is not just desired, but is paramount to success. Our product involves human lives. We cannot be satisfied with the mediocre, for anything less than <u>quality care</u> is failure. To achieve quality, all staff and managers must become *excited* - viewing their role as important, their contributions as valued and their involvement as crucial. That *excitement* is the key to our success.

You may say that this is idealistic. Not all staff can perform at the same level of ability. Some are more capable than others. There is no disputing that we all have different strengths and abilities. One mitigating factor ensures success - the manager is responsible to illicit from each person his/her <u>maximum</u> performance.

The only way that staff will give their all is when they are *excited* about what they do. When *excitement* exists, a person becomes self motivated and self-managed to do the best to his/her ability. Our primary and best asset within our organizations is the people who work there. They represent the lion's share of the budget. It is their efforts that determines the organization's effectiveness. Investing in our people to get them *excited* ensures our success.

To the second question - "Why long term care?" An immediate response by some will be - "Is not management the same regardless of the setting?" Here my bias appears. I do not dispute that management concepts and techniques are universal. What I am implying is that those in long term care have specific differences.

There is no disputing that all organizations strive for quality. The difference in our specialty is that the quality we strive to achieve cannot be easily defined or measured. We attempt to achieve an enormous goal called quality of life - an intangible, highly individualized, and at times an almost immeasurable objective.

We have in our midst a normal adult (who has experienced more years than you and I have as yet lived) who like us has the need to control his life and be independent to determine the course of his destiny. An adult who has become frail and in need of assistance in the later part of his life. This person is one who:

- has not been mentally handicapped from birth, experiencing only institutionalization as the mainstay of his existence.
- has not been psychologically unstable where institutionalization is needed to direct his appropriate existence.
- is not a short term patient who has one major problem that needs rectifying.

He is *you* and *I* - only <u>older</u> - who has experienced a series of crisis that forces him now to move to an institutional setting for the remainder of his life.

Our industry has changed dramatically within the last two decades. We have taken in a more complex and demanding clientele. We have been required to develop new and creative skills and programs. We have in a few short years sky rocketed into a specialty that is probably the most growing on this continent. We as managers have been forced to:

⇒ modernize our specialty in leaps and bounds.
⇒ bring sophistication into our environment and techniques.
⇒ motivate and direct staff with limited training to care for some individuals who would tax the skills of the most skilled therapist.

Long term care is undergoing an industry-wide revolution. Yet we are required to do all of that with limited resources, untrained staff, unclear mandates, antiquated equipment and buildings, and a newly developing and highly challenging focus on resident rights. We are so busy moving ahead, that unfortunately our pace has left a number of facilities straggling behind.

That has created two distinct groups of long term care settings. There are those who have achieved quality care. Progressive organizations who have learned to be efficient with their available resources. They have become the forerunners and pace setters who have established new and innovative ideas for the industry.

Then there is the other group. Long term care settings who have stuck to the "old ways" of managing. They have been delinquent in keeping up with the knowledge, trends, and expectations of their specialty. Instead, they have been caught in the techniques and philosophies of the past, trying desperately to get into present day. Facilities where everything has changed, yet nothing is different. At this time, they are truly struggling to keep their organizations together, let alone provide quality care.

Knowing which management concepts and techniques can be made to fit the variety of needs of either setting becomes the challenge. The manager of long term care must be able to identify the specific and unique forces within his setting in order to mold the necessary components that will allow the leaders to take one step forward and the trailers one step closer. If that cannot be done, then it is the staff providing the care who will become confused and lost in the movement.

It is important at this time to identify the mainstay of this text. There exists a significant relationship regarding care and staff -

The level of care the staff gives to the resident is totally reflected by how well the facility takes care of its staff.

It is the foundation on which quality of life is built that dictates its success. It is one thing to look at the person, but another to look at the environment in which that person must work or live. Programs are not the issue. Short-sighted managers who merely insert a program they see progressive facilities using, accomplish nothing more than to increase the quantity, not the quality of what is offered.

Quality of life is a philosophy that is difficult to measure and hard to administer, but most certainly experienced.

Until an organization has crossed the threshold to clearly understand its role and been provided the freedom to create its own autonomy, the goals for the staff and more importantly for the residents will always be illusive.

Yes management concepts are the same, but there is a difference in long term care that creates a uniqueness. This book deals with that difference and the needs it creates.

THE FOCUS OF THIS BOOK

Managing others in any setting can be a difficult undertaking for some. It is a constant struggle of trying to get others to reach what seems to be a common goal. At times seeming to encounter constant frustrations of moving three steps ahead and two back. One that has an overwhelming need to pursue further knowledge and skills to handle the complex and ever changing dynamics of the work place.

The challenge for any manager is to find the problem that prevents him from being that successful manager. At times we would like to believe that the solution to our problems is a simple one - identify the people creating the problem (whether staff or our bosses) and get rid of them and it will be solved. If only it were so simple. Just as there can be no one solution or technique in managing, there is usually much more than one mitigating factor creating the chaos that can sometimes be encountered. Now to the limitations of this text.

In my book entitled <u>Working with the Frail Elderly</u>, I discuss the cognitively well, physically disabled older client. That text presents three client responses - the well adjusted, the aggressive and the withdrawn/apathetic. These concepts have become highly popular in understanding the "why" of many resident behaviors. In my later book The Tactics of Supportive Therapy: Effective Intervention Strategies on Caring for the Alzheimer's Victim, I created the analogy of mental impairment to being lost. Again its success has been impressive. Many have found they can more clearly understand this clientele and their behavior through that description and the related interventions.

Each book identified its limitations. There are more than three responses to the cognitively well, physically disabled resident than what I generalized. There is more to Alzheimer's and related disorders than being lost. However, the descriptions have been valuable to many staff and families working with the elderly.

There are similar limitations in this text. There is no attempt here to expand on theory or challenge the theorists in their perceptions. Instead what has been done in this text is to take a very complex process and attempt to place it in the very practical, day-by-day experiences of long term care. Almost all of what you will read has been presented to a large variety of health care managers and staff in numerous seminars in recent years. The result of that presentation has been an enthusiastic response, a statement by those attending - "after hearing you, I understand more clearly the problems I create and the problems I must deal with." The request has been made to put it into a book. To those who have asked for it, here it is.

As in any work such as this, the material is presented in a progressive manner. Each page and chapter builds on the last. Chapter two identifies the number and variety of problems that can face any manager in any facility. It establishes that no matter what your management abilities, the organization in which you work can either hamper or enhance your skills. Then in chapter three we identify interdepartmental relations. This chapter centers on only three very general management descriptions - the effective manager, those who are managed and those who must manage - and their impact throughout the organization. Chapter four discusses three general groups of staff - the positive, the average and the negative and expands on the resulting staff dynamics and affects of peer pressure.

The fifth chapter draws the two groups together. It demonstrates the impact of the previously described management styles and management dynamics with those of the defined staff characteristics and conflicts. What is outlined in this chapter defines the organization's milieu and how it can effect resident care and quality of life. In this chapter you will be required to examine the effectiveness of your own organization. Presented is a questionnaire entitled "The Staff Needs Assessment." It will challenge you to scrutinize the staff supports and philosophy that exists within your facility.

The next three chapters discuss the interventions both at a personal as well as an organizational level. These chapters expand on each issue identified in the Staff Needs Assessment questionnaire and how they relate to the dynamics described in the first four chapters. Chapter six discusses management assertiveness and personal management skills. Chapter seven and eight examine ways to enhance organizational communication and problem solving. Chapter nine provides available options in establishing an effective and flexible recognition system and techniques to creative an effective staff education program.

In chapter ten, we will establish how the material presented in this book can assist you. This final chapter requires you to evaluate your performance as a manager and to decide your personal plan of action to deal with problems you experience within your organization.

What is attempted in these pages is to personalize management in long term care. The focus is not centered on theory, but on the core, the heart of what may be creating our frustrations. Yet, it is important to admit in this text, what I admitted in my other two books - everything you are about to read is a *lie*. <u>Don't stop reading</u>.

Management and organizational dynamics are broad and complex topics. Thousands of books have been written with as many variations as there are writers in describing management dynamics and interventions. This book does not attempt to replace those, nor does it attempt to say that all that is presented here is exactly as it is described. There are no such absolutes. Just as there is more to our cognitively well residents than three responses, or more to Alzheimer's than being lost, the lies here are simple - there is more to management than three descriptive abilities, more to staff than three levels of performance. As you read, you need to broaden your scope beyond what is on these pages, using the material presented to enhance your own perception of what is happening and what is needed.

Now to the caution. I know of no way to set clear imagery, other than to be specific in defining potential examples about people and their actions. To isolate two pages from the entire text, allows anyone to easily distort and take out of context whatever is desired, but it will be inaccurate. If you are out to justify a belief that you may have about administrators, then you may be able to confirm that if you isolate specific examples defined in these pages. By reading one of the scenarios describing how an ineffective administrator can cause the nurse manager endless problems, it is easy to make the conclusion "See, I was right, I always said administrators were like that. I was right, it is all their fault." The results of this type of selective analysis can be compared to the experience of watching a play. As soon as you see the first character that appears to be the villain, you do not walk out saying "I know who is the culprit." If you did you might be sorry you missed the entire play when you learn that your quick judgment was inaccurate and the "who done it" was someone completely different.

In this book, every position, every level of the organization is examined. As we discuss the frustrations created by a poor administrator, we also discuss the impact of a poorly functioning board, an incompetent director of resident care and an ineffective unit manager. Criticism is not directed toward the position, but the people who hold that position. As in a play, the characters and plot cannot unfold in the first few moments of scene one. Each player is an intricate part of the drama. Each role intertwines with the other to create the suspense of the story. Likewise the content of this text cannot be construed from a certain phrase or page. You must go from beginning to end in order to reach your conclusions.

Lastly, this is not a passive book which will allow you to just read the material presented. In a sense you will not only be watching the play, but you will be on the stage. This participatory style of writing requires you to be involved in this text in order to gain the most from the material presented. The questions, scenarios and exercises are designed to put you through a mental process which will allow you to analyze more effectively what you are experiencing and what you need to do to allow you to move one more step closer to becoming that manager you desire.

Like any play, the goal is to get you *excited*. To get you *excited* about what you are reading. Get you *excited* about what you do. Get you *excited* about what you can do more effectively.

Let us begin!
The curtain is now rising.
Your role is set.
On with the drama.

Chapter Two

WHERE'S THE PROBLEM

To be an effective manager, one must be proficient in three areas of performance.

1) An effective *people manager* - able to work with those around you, motivate them to get them excited, tap their strengths and work to eliminate their weakness.

2) An effective *organizational manager* - organizing and creating the tools these people need to do their job well, which includes an effective communication process, assessment mechanism, mapping of paper, scheduling tasks, etc.

3) An effective *resource manager* - able to use the dollars, equipment and physical environment to their full capacity.

Unfortunately, some managers may be skilled in one area and weak in another. This can create a diversity in management performance. Some managers may know what they want to do but have trouble getting it done. Others may know how to do it, but don't know what to do. Still others may know how and what to do, but are in an organization that does not support them in doing it.

To describe these responses more effectively, imagine that managing is like pushing a wheel-barrow (*figure #1*).

⇒ The wheel of the wheel-barrow represents the staff - those who complete the work and translate the manager's efforts to move it forward.

⇒ The load in the wheel-barrow represents the goals, objectives, staff supports, etc. - those things that reflect the profile of the organization.

⇒ The manager's ability to lift the load and move it forward represents his skills in knowing the job and motivating and directing her staff.

Organizational Supports

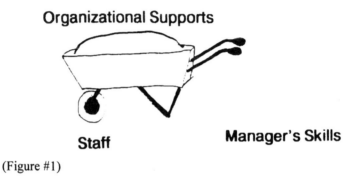

Staff   **Manager's Skills**

(Figure #1)

Let us examine the problems that can exist:

1) The Manager Who Lacks The People Skills

Some managers know what they want to do but have trouble getting it done. This is the manager who lacks the people skills and is weak in motivating and directing others. She is probably an excellent nurse. Her organizational skills in providing the things needed to do the job are strong (charting process, care conferencing methods, assessment tools, etc.). Her resource management skills are also superb. Unfortunately, she lacks the people skills necessary to motivate her staff to do the job. For her, management is like pushing a wheel-barrow with a flat tire (*figure #2*). She has the ability to lift it (the technical knowledge of what needs to be done in her department or on her unit) and a realistic load (appropriate organizational demands and supports), but has a flat tire (staff involvement and morale is low). As a result, she finds it is very difficult to move forward. This is the profile of the Manager Who Must Manage discussed in the following chapter.

(Figure #2)

Organizational Supports

Low Staff Morale   **Manager's Skills**

2) Managers Who Lack the Technical Knowledge

Others know how to do it, but don't know what to do. This is the manager who is liked by all. She works hard to develop a strong, friendly and honest relationship, but does not know how to steer the energy into getting the job done. She has very good people skills, but lacks in her organizational and resource management ability. She has difficulty setting realistic goals and objectives because she does not understand her role. As a manager, she lacks the skills or knowledge to be effective. Those who work for her are confused and frustrated about the direction she establishes. In this case the wheel-barrow is intact (*figure #3*) - good load (the organizational demands and supports are realistic), a round, firm tire (effective people skills in developing an open and trusting relationship), but the person pushing it hasn't the strength or ability to lift it to get it to go anywhere (lack of technical skills as a manager or a long term care nurse). This is the profile of the Manager Who is Managed.

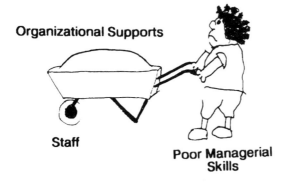

Organizational Supports

Staff

Poor Managerial Skills

(Figure #3)

3) Managers Who Lack Realistic Organizational Supports

Others know how and what to do but are in an organization that does not support them in doing it. This is the effective manager who has strong people, organizational and resource management ability, but is not allowed or is even hampered in her freedom to use them. She simply cannot fully accomplish what she wants because the setting in which she works does not support her. She has the necessary people skills - excellent communicator and staff motivator - and the needed technical knowledge (a thorough understanding of the resident as well as her role as manager). The problem lies in the demands placed on her. This person encounters underlying factors within the organization that she has little authority to change - poor organizational communication, no consistency in management, responsibility without authority, limited staff or environmental resources, inconsistent support by upper management, a lack of accountability, etc.

The weight of the existing problems requires this manager to invest considerable time and energy to move her staff only a few steps forward. In our wheel-barrow scenario (*figure #4*), this manager has the ability to lift the wheel-barrow (technical knowledge both as a manager and nurse) and could move it forward (people knowledge on how to direct and motivate others and establish an open and trusting relationship) but is hampered by the weight she is being asked to carry. The load is unrealistic (inappropriate organizational goals and supports). This is the impact on an effective manager when management is not supported within the organization.

Staff morale and trust within such a setting is always debased. Each time this manager tries to revitalize and involve her staff, she is countered by forces initiated by individuals beyond her control. In order to move the wheel-barrow, she must continually re-inflate the tire, knowing that in a short time the heavy weight from the load will eventually flatten it again.

Movement forward for this manger is exhausting given the amount of energy required to go only a few steps. Many good managers stay only a few years in such a facility due to the pressures experienced. When this person leaves, it is in frustration and disappointment. She believes that little of what she planned was accomplished. In actual fact, given the weight of what had to be overcome and the difficulties encountered, this individual carried the organization a considerable distance.

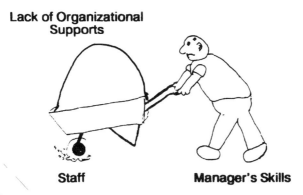

Lack of Organizational Supports

Staff   **Manager's Skills**

(Figure #4)

4) The Effective Manager

The effective manager (*figure #5*) is a manager who is comfortable at all three levels - people management, organizational management and resource management. She has the necessary people skills to excite staff and maintain high morale (round, firm tire) and the appropriate technical skills as a manager and as a long term care nurse (strength and ability to lift the wheel-barrow and set it in the desired direction), in a facility with clearly defined goals, and adequate resources and supports (a realistic, well balanced load). The result is a wheel-barrow that gets to its destination

Organizational Supports

Staff   **Manager's Skills**

(FIGURE #5)

THE IDEAL ORGANIZATION

The "ideal" organization is not always one that has *everything*. There are many facilities which appear to have less than the "ideal" - a poor staff/resident ratio, an older building, limited equipment - yet staff still provide excellent care and have high morale. In this organization staff and managers alike are excited to work there. In such a setting, the staff supports created seem to compensate for the lack of physical resources.

On the other hand, there are facilities that seem to have "everything" - a new modern building, higher than normal staff/resident ratio, sophisticated and plentiful equipment, available resources, yet the care and morale is deplorable. In these organizations, staff and managers seem paralyzed and in some instances self destructive. These settings lacks the people element needed to get staff and managers excited about what they do and where they do it.

The challenge for any manager, regardless of where that person works, is to determine -

What do I need to do to be effective in managing those under my supervision?

How must the organization in which we work be structured in order to support those doing their job, whether staff or manager?

The ability to successfully answer these challenges depends on one's skill in defining the problems blocking one's way and then identifying what is needed to resolve them.

WHERE IS THE PROBLEM?

Take a moment to give thought to the following question:

What chronic problems or difficulties do you experience as a manager?

The answer to this question is not easy. There is no doubt that a number of things immediately come to mind. I am sure that if you spent any time considering your answer, you would probably create quite an extensive list.

The problems facing any manager can come from a number of sources. Let us examine these in specific categories. In later chapters we will detail each area, the impact they have on organizational dynamics and how to resolve them.

IS THE PROBLEM PSYCHOLOGICAL?

Whenever one or more persons are gathered together you have the potential of encountering specific psychological forces. Organizations are no different. Some of the difficulties experienced by managers may be related to specific psychological dynamics.

1) STAFFING DYNAMICS

In any work place there exists a specific combination of forces and pressures playing on each staff member to influence how that person should act or even think. Each work environment has its own culture, its own standards of conduct. This culture can result in a simple, yet significant fact:

There can be more pressure staff-on-staff than managers-on-staff in many organizations.

It doesn't matter whether the company is building cars, selling clothes or caring for the frail elderly, the dynamics that exist in each setting become the playing field. Staffing dynamics are an integral component that the manager must understand and constantly adjust to in order to achieve the desired quality and performance from the workers within.

These dynamics and how they impact on managers and the organization will be discussed in detail in chapter four.

2) GROUP DYNAMICS

Interesting things seem to happen to an individual when placed in a group. A multitude of books and research papers have expounded on the impact of group pressure from sports to riots to organizational dynamics. You may see or hear different responses from a person when he interacts with you alone versus when he is a member of a group.

Mary, a fellow manager approaches you in the hallway just before an important meeting. She takes you aside and says "That topic you have on the agenda, I'm behind you 100%. If you need any help selling it, just give me the high sign." You enter the meeting; your controversial issue is presented; you raise your concerns; throughout the discussion you are struggling, finding yourself on a hot seat that only gets hotter. No matter what you say, you find you can't get any approval or support. Throughout the meeting Mary sits there listening. You give her the high sign, the low sign and any other sign you can think of, but she does not respond. After the meeting you are sweating and deflated and Mary approaches you in the hall saying "Too bad it wasn't accepted. I was behind you 100%!"

The forces of group pressure can influence any of us. These dynamics become the foundation on which staff and management dynamics are built.

3) GAME PLAYING

Psychological games are often unconscious patterns of behavior which on the surface communicate one thing but when completed achieve another, more deviant outcome. A psychological game creates a win/lose situation. It is where one person is often taken off balance, not knowing what exactly happened, but conscious of the outcome. Psychological games represent situations where a person is repeatedly manipulated, causing him to become angry or experience bad feelings.

It is important to note that the incidence of psychological game playing is very much influenced by the individuals involved and the people and circumstances around that person. Those most likely to initiate psychological games are individuals with a weak self image, who find it necessary to satisfy personal needs in a devious manner. Likewise, the only people this individual will be able to "hook" into a psychological game are:

⇒ others with a weak self image
⇒ those with a set and restrictive personality quality (i.e. strong nurturers or rescuers who feel compelled to help)
⇒ individuals who are in a strained or negative relationship (i.e. organizations with poor staff/management morale).

Psychological games are not for "fun." They have three very specific desired outcomes: they <u>reinforce an individual's belief system</u>, <u>gain recognition</u>, and <u>establish power</u>.

The person initiating the game often believes that his/her actions are justified and appropriate given the circumstances encountered. You will find that much of the discussion in the following chapters on management and staff dynamics reflects game playing. In Eric Berne's book <u>Games People Play</u>, he outlines a multitude of games with a variety of themes. Here is a summary of a few common ones as they may apply to a long term care facility:

a) "I'm Only Stupid" or "Kick Me"

This is the person who tries hard but never succeeds. Let me demonstrate. As my boss, you give me a job to do. The instructions are detailed and clear. There is no obvious reason for me not to perform to the expected standard. I try the task but do not accomplish it properly. The next day you give me another job. Again, I don't complete the task as expected. Eventually you are placed in the situation of having to confront me on my poor performance. Once confronted I now approach others and say "Look how hard I tried, she reprimanded me anyway."

This game is frequently initiated by a person with a poor self image - an individual who throughout his life has been constantly "put down" regardless of how he has performed. Being told, either directly or indirectly, that everything you do is wrong can result in the belief that you are "stupid" or incompetent. This creates an expectation that every situation encountered will result in failure, convincing him to invest only a minimal amount ability and energy. The outcome of this decision is to fail, which only reinforces his negative perception of himself. The cycle repeats itself again and again.

The game is not over yet. Once feeling *slighted* from the manager's confrontation, this staff member approaches others during coffee break and states "That manager is something else. Just because I didn't do what she wanted the first time, she said that I was stupid. Can you believe that? She said I was stupid. I am so upset." The game must draw in a strong nurturer or rescuer to allow it to be successful. Rescuers are people who cannot stand seeing someone "upset." Once a rescuer is "hooked," that person will side with the victim, *even though the rescuer does not know all of the facts about the incident in question.* The rescuer's comment "That is not fair. She didn't need to say that to you. Don't let it get you down." The win for the game player is obvious, he has successfully gained recognition for failing.

The game is still not over. To make it complete, it is necessary for the game player to gain power as well. If the rescuer acquires personal satisfaction by protecting the down trodden, she may take further action. The rescuer will decide to approach the initial manager on behalf of the victim (but remember, not at the request of the victim). The rescuer accosts that manager saying "Why did you call that staff member stupid?" The original manager's response "What did I do?" The manager who confronted the original staff member cannot understand how she became the "bad guy" in dealing with a staff member who was not performing his job.

There is no doubt that certain psychological games will decrease in effectiveness over time. Games begin to break down when people get tired of the victim. In this game, many realize that this person *always* complains about how others treat him, no matter what is said or done. Their frequent contact with the victim may demonstrate that his work performance is poor and many of the comments are valid. When the victim discovers that the response by others decreases in intensity, he will usually target only a select few (typically those who themselves gain recognition by playing the "rescuer"). This game describes the actions of the R*escuer* and *Dead Wood* detailed in the following chapters and becomes the basis for some of the cliques that develop within the organization.

b) "Let's You and Him Fight"

This game is frequently played by an employee who believes *all* managers are ineffective. This game begins when an employee approaches a manager and states "Alice, *I don't usually do this*, <u>but</u> I just can't let it go by without telling you. Did you hear what Heather said about you?" The employee then reconstructs an exaggerated account of negative comments supposedly said by another manager about Alice.

Later that same employee approaches Heather, "Heather, *I don't usually do this*, <u>but</u> I just can't let it go by without telling you. Do you know what Alice said about you?" This manager is told of an exaggerated account of negative comments Alice supposedly said about Heather.

Neither manager knows that the employee has talked to the other or that what was stated was probably distorted, possibly even fabricated. This employee will only initiate this game when it is possible to involve two managers who already have a strained relationship. The intention is to further deteriorate their professional relationship, thereby decreasing their ability to work together effectively. The employee can then justify his belief that manager's are ineffective.

The game must satisfy the other needs of gaining power and recognition to be fully successful. Even though this employee may see himself as "only a staff member," he has created a situation that effectively neutralizes the power of two managers. This outcome will only be achieved if these managers play along by not checking with the other what was said and why.

At the same time, this employee has potentially increased the bond between himself and <u>each</u> manager. Telling each what supposedly was heard, gives the impression that he is looking out for their best interests by warning them of what has occurred. This describes well the behavior of the *Saboteur* in the later section on staffing dynamics.

c) "Bitching" or "Ain't It Awful"

Individuals who participate in this game believe that everything within the organization is negative and <u>unsolvable</u>. This person takes a flaw or weakness and exaggerates it well out of proportion. Their frequent comments include: "This place stinks. They don't give a damn about us. No one listens. . . ." Everything this person presents is always in absolutes. To him, there are few exceptions that are positive and even those are viewed with suspicion.

This negativity can develop for a number of reasons. It may stem from the person's chronic negative view of his life, himself and his future - he has never seen the positive in anything. The "skill" in finding the "negative" results in his workplace being approached no differently.

Another reason for negativity is from the person who feels stuck in a job that he does not enjoy. His dissatisfaction is always reflected in his comments. It can also develop in a person who has felt emotionally "hurt" where he works. His unwillingness to forget what has occurred, colors his perception of the workplace.

The employee who "bitches" chronically does not look for solutions to the problems identified. He only uses these as an opportunity for personal gain. If during coffee break someone responds to his complaining by saying - "That is a good point, how do you think it could be resolved?," the "bitcher" would probably move to another table.

The desired outcome of this game is to reinforce this person's beliefs. To continually profess that where you work "stinks," justifies that the job you perform can "stink." It legitimizes the poor level of job performance by this person. You have invariably heard the comment from this type of staff member - "If they don't give a damn about me, then *I am not going to do any more than I have to.*"

To change this person's perception of his work setting is not easy. Professing that staff in the organization are respected, involved, and seen as important is to force this person to change his view. That ultimately will require him to admit that the problem is not where he works but himself.

In fact, this person is in constant fear that he may be contradicted. His response to those who attempt to get people excited and solve problems within the organization is to make them the target of his "bitching." Many staff and even some managers can be afraid of this individual. To get on the wrong side of this person by challenging or contradicting him can result in almost anything and everything being said about you. Any staff member or manager who lacks confidence can be easily influenced by the "bitcher's tongue."

In fact, there is a more devious and even more powerful outcome from the bitcher's actions. He has the ability to take staff who come to work excited about what they are doing, and where they are doing it and deflate them by his constant "nattering in their ear." Not only does he not like his job, he can make it so others dislike their jobs as well. That is power.

Finally, there is no question that the "bitcher" gains recognition from his actions. When a group sits with this person and does not challenge him, they are left to listen to his "bitching." He is the center of attention. When he is quiet, there is no attention paid to him.

The effects of this game is to weaken trust and morale within an organization. This aptly describes the impact of negative staff discussed in the section on staffing dynamics.

d) "Yes, But . . ."

This game often involves staff who have "burned out" - those who no longer enjoy where they work or what they do, or those who are in a job beyond their competency level. Playing this game creates for others a psychological *merry-go-round*. No matter what is suggested, the person playing "Yes, but . . ." will always find a reason why it won't work. The most common response heard by the person using this game is "*Yes* that's a good idea, *but* we tried something like that 10 years ago. It didn't work." The resultant decision - "isn't worth trying anything like that again."

The person who has "burned out" no longer believes that anything will change to the positive. He has convinced himself that the problems exist not because he has given up, but simply because they cannot be solved. This view creates a self-fulfilling prophecy - constant blocking or resisting change, means that change will not occur. Unfortunately, to allow someone else to resolve something that you have continually said cannot be solved challenges your ability - if she could solve it why couldn't you? Blocking every solution is proving that one's evaluation is accurate. This perception will be detailed in our discussion of the *Structured Staff* and *Dead Wood* in staffing dynamics and the *Manager who is Managed* in management dynamics.

e) "Now I've got you, you S.O.B."

Imagine that we are two managers who do not get along. You are the unit manager for the afternoon shift and I am the unit manager for the day shift. For some reason or another, I hold a grudge against you about something you did in the past. I have learned to keep score in a relationship, always feeling justified to retaliate for any "hurts" experienced. Unfortunately my score keeping and retaliation is influence by my insecurities and over sensitivity created by a weak self image. When something occurs, I always exaggerate the actions and intentions of others. For me, "getting even" means that I must "out do" the original "hurt."

On my shift, the director of resident care explains a new policy to be implemented. She spends considerable time detailing that policy and instructs me to pass the information to the next manager on duty. And that is you. When you begin your shift, I hand you the policy and tell you to read it. Nothing more. Within days the full impact of the policy and your lack of knowledge regarding the details places you in an awkward and possibly foolish position. The result is a decrease in your effectiveness and a feeling that "I have gotten even."

The game is not over. To be complete, the person must gain power and recognition as well. In response to what was encountered, you tell the director of resident care that you were not given the information. She then questions me. As in many games, I will play on any weakness within the relationship. If the director of resident care is not a confident manager and you are assertive, she probably feels threatened by you. My response to the director of resident care would be "You know what she is like! She only listens to what she wants. I think that between the two of us we can help her to overcome that." This feeds well into what the director of resident care needs - to learn how to deal with you. From that point on, whenever you make a comment at a meeting, you notice the director of resident care and this manager looking at each other and smiling. You are suspicious, but can't understand what it all means. This describes well the behaviors of the *Saboteur* and the *Manager who is Managed.*

Psychological games will eventually sour. As time passes, the payoffs or desired outcomes are not as easily acquired. This requires the person to either switch to another game or intensify the original one in order to illicit the desired response. In the game *Let's You and Him Fight* for example - the person will use the line "I don't always do this" too many times. After awhile, others start to catch on and say - "I've heard him say that before." The game player can intensify the game by attempting to "hook" someone in upper management, send a negative letter to the editor of the local newspaper about the problems within the organization, or approach a board member on the sly. The target manager can now find herself answering questions to stronger forces then the mere "rescuer."

Generally if game playing is allowed to continue without being challenged, then the impact on the organization will deteriorate staff/management relationships, create a feeling of mistrust, waste time and energies, and prevent effective problem solving.

Many of the intervention strategies presented in upcoming chapters target game playing specifically. To counter games the manager must be able to:

1) Identify, analyze and satisfy an individual's desired outcomes (need for recognition and power) in order to avoid the need to initiate games.
2) Develop the skills to challenge the game player.
3) Set in motion a clearly defined problem solving and communication mechanism making games difficult to maintain.
4) Establish a strong recognition system that eliminates the need for games.

Chapters six, seven, eight and nine provide a number of interventions to help you in working towards these objectives.

IS THE PROBLEM ORGANIZATIONAL?

Organizational problems reflects the setting where the manager is required to work. If the tools needed to do the job are not in place, or the manager hasn't the freedom nor support to implement them, or allowed to adapt the situation to accommodate their lacking, then her hands are tied. Her effectiveness in managing her staff is diluted.

1) Staff Supports

If the appropriate supports are not there for the managers or staff to do their job, then it won't be done. The premise that the level of care the staff gives to the resident is reflective of how well the facility takes care of its staff highlights specific components of an organizational management philosophy. These are *Permission, Accountability* and *Recognition*.

a) Permission

Permission is a philosophy that states - "I hired you to do a job, therefore go and do it." This philosophy expresses that each employee, whether staff or manager, knows his job and if provided the freedoms has the ability and desire to perform it effectively. It springs from a basis of trust - a belief that all staff and managers will complete their job to the best of their ability.

Permission encourages staff to *think.*

It allows staff the freedom to determine what they need to do in order to perform their care, routines and duties well.

Without *permission* an organization implies that staff and managers will only perform their job if they are closely monitored and supervised. This philosophy requires the setting to be structured, where everything is scheduled and developed within a strict routine to ensure that all tasks and duties are completed. The effect of consistently telling people what to do is to encourage them *not to think.* In such a facility, staff hold the belief that they are not trusted and their only value is "from the neck down" - technicians rather than caregivers. Their lack of involvement in the decision making process and the workings of the organization squelches ownership. When they are not part of the process, things are only done when they are told to do them. Lack of ownership, results in little commitment and enthusiasm. It stifles excitement.

b) Accountability

This second part of the philosophy concerns accountability. It states - "If you don't do your job, you will hear about it." Without accountability there can be little consistency. When staff and/or managers are allowed to do what they please regardless of what is established, nothing remains but chaos.

Lack of accountability and its effects can best be demonstrated with the resident care plan. If you have noticed the following in your facility, then accountability is probably lacking:

> *If the cognitively well residents at the change of shift are watching the entrance to the unit to see who is coming on duty, so they know what they can do or what they can have.*

When accountably is lacking, staff have the freedom to do what they want regardless of what the team establishes. When specific expectations are not adhered to and guidelines are not maintained, there is nothing left but confusion. This causes each shift to have different demands and freedoms for each resident.

If staff are allowed to do something inappropriate without any actions taken by management to correct or end it, then do not blame those staff. People will do what they believe is right, or for some what they can get away with, until they are corrected. Likewise, do not blame the staff member's peers. *Staff cannot make staff accountable unless managers make staff accountable.* If a manager is not able or willing to make staff accountable, then do not fault that manager either. Look to the manager's manager. Accountability starts at the top.

c) Recognition

This final component of the effective manager's philosophy states "when you do something well, you will hear about it." Without recognition for one's accomplishments it becomes difficult to maintain one's enthusiasm and drive.

Imagine if you spent considerable time and energy developing and implementing a solution to a long standing problem within your facility. Once the solution is initiated, it has immediate benefits for all staff and residents. Afterwards, no one says a word to you about what you have done. How would that influence your enthusiasm to tackle the next problem?

There seems to be a chronic weakness within the health care industry:

Rarely do we hear when we do anything well, but we seem to always hear when we "screw up."

Lack of recognition in the workplace can drain any caregiver's emotions and energies. It paralyzes rather than excites.

We will discuss in detail the need for staff and management supports. Without these needs being satisfied, everyone's ability to do their job well within the organization will be affected. In our wheelbarrow scenario it is similar to flattening the tire. It is difficult to move a wheelbarrow forward when the tire is flat.

2) Resources and Workload

An effective way to assess a facility is to spend a few days on the unit as though you were a resident living there. Personalizing any experience is a valuable mechanism to uncover what is happening and why. When I assess a facility, I will eat with the residents, sit with them in the lounge, attend activities with them, and even have staff put me in the tub (I will have my clothes on). In this manner I not only know what the residents are experiencing, but the staff as well.

In one facility I noticed an obvious problem. The tub room was too small to get a lift through the tub room door. The bottom of the door way and the door itself were chewed away from the number of times the legs of the lift hit them. To understand what was encountered, I asked a staff member to place me in the tub using a lift.

The staff member on the first two tries didn't hit that tub room door at the *exact* angle. Each time she hit the door frame, she was required to back up and try again. Once in the tub room, the challenges did not stop there. The tub was located too close to the wall. This required her to creep the lift behind the tub inch by inch, jiggling it into the tight space between the wall and the back of the tub. Once in place, she lowered me into the tub. The tub was at floor level. The height of the tub meant that she would have to work on her hands and knees if she were to wash me.

That <u>may be</u> tolerable if it were done only once a week. Unfortunately, staff were required to do it forty-five times a week or more (based on the number of residents on that unit), fifty-two weeks of the year (two thousand, three hundred and forty times per year).

After the experience, I approached the administrator. I asked if he was aware of the problems staff had while bathing frail residents. He said that he was. I asked why the tub was not adapted to accommodate the lift. He responded that there was "no money in the budget to do anything about it at this time." I queried further, asking how long he had been aware of this problem. His response was "years." When asked why it was not budgeted, he said "Money is tight. It is not a priority." Whose priority?

For most direct line staff, it is not the major "organizational issues" that are the priority, it is what some managers may consider the "little things." These "little things" can better be called:

Mosquito Annoyances - initially tolerable problems that occur over and over again until they develop into a very frustrating and annoying situation.

It was not surprising that on the unit just described, staff morale and enthusiasm was low. The amount of time and energy wasted on this one simple task created considerable frustrations.

I wouldn't let this issue go. I asked the administrator where his office phone was located. He was puzzled by my question, but answered "On my desk." I told him that I wanted to have his phone removed from his desk and made into a wall phone by his office door. Furthermore, he was not allowed any writing surface anywhere near that phone. We discussed the impact this simple change would have on him each time his phone rang. At the sound of the ring, he would be required to get up from his desk to answer the call. If he needed to write something down while on the phone, he would have to let the phone dangle; go to his desk; get writing paper and a pen; return to the phone; do some interesting contortions to balance the phone, hold the paper and write. I asked him a few questions: How much time would he waste given the frequency his phone rings? How frustrated would he become? How long would he allow the phone to stay there? I think he got my point.

How can any manager effectively keep staff excited when it is impossible for staff: to get a resident's wheelchair through a bathroom door; to encourage a resident to be independent when there are no adaptive devices (specialized forks, knives and spoons, etc.); to bathe residents in a tub room that lacks a proper heating and cooling system (the room is sweltering on the hottest days and freezing during the coldest); when there is a chronic shortage of towels; etc. Such a setting professes quality of life, but does not provide staff the tools needed to achieve it or adapt their routine to accommodate it. It is not easy for staff or managers to do a job when the basics of what they need are lacking or the freedom to work around the nuisance is not provided.

3) Education

Imagine the impact on any industry that ignored staff training. Take the example of a company that changes from the standard welding line operated by human welders to a modern line of robotic welders. In this fictitious company, it is believed by the managers that standard welders should be able to handle and maintain the robotic equipment without any further training. Their philosophy is "welding is welding."

Their welders are simply given the robots and told to complete the job. There is no doubt that the inevitable will happen. At some point, an untrained operator will push the wrong button. This will result in his damaging the machine, or worse, injuring himself. In any event, it will be the workplace and its managers who will be held responsible for their negligence should either occur.

Education is the key to quality care. The clientele in long term care has changed dramatically over the last twenty years. In 1974, we had a fairly ambulatory, generally independent resident population, with an average age of seventy-four years old. By the late 1980's, the average age of the resident population of long term care sky rocketed to eight-seven years old. The 1990's has introduced us to the "new resident."

Admissions now include two very different types of resident profiles. Those who are cognitively well, physically disabled are now generally very old and very frail. The length of their stay within the organization is relatively short compared to the resident of the past. Staff now find themselves caring for an individual who has encountered dramatic change and whose quality of life is difficult to define and implement without specific skills. However, it is the other type who is even more challenging - the confused and disoriented elderly.

The mentally impaired elderly are the most complex client that our organizations have ever encountered. The care strategies and interventions utilized by long term care with the cognitively well resident are no longer applicable. Each mentally impaired resident is individualized in his strengths, abilities, symptoms and needs. If care is not specifically geared to the needs of the individual, then behavioral challenges such as aggressive outbursts will be constant.

Most of my present clinical work with long term care facilities now centers on care strategies for the mentally impaired resident. It is amazing the number of staff who know little of the diseases causing this behavior and of the care that is required to be successful. Not unlike the example about the robotic welders, staff in many facilities have simply been thrust into a situation where they are expected to understand what to do and how to do it with little knowledge of what is involved. The result is that staff are being injured by the chronic aggressive outbursts of this clientele, or the clientele is being over medicated and restrained because the staff lack the understanding to uncover and employ other more effective intervention strategies.

Without understanding the "why," staff are left with the ability to only perform a superficial analysis. Not understanding this resident's condition and situation means that appropriate solutions evade them. Without formal and consistent training, staff will be unable "to think" for themselves when encountering resident behavior that is out of their norm. This sets the stage for two possible results. One requires the nurse manager to continually "think" for her staff - defining for every staff member on each shift how to meet each resident's needs repeatedly. Any manager encountering this demand would become harried, unable to meet the needs successfully. This leads to crisis intervention rather than problem solving, requiring the situations that are the most serious to take precedent. A process of constantly moving from one crisis to another. It is only when the resident "explodes" that he becomes a priority, requiring a major investment of time and energy.

Long term care is more complicated now than it has ever been. Unfortunately, few of our staff, and in many cases managers as well, have received more than basic training in the areas of gerontology, geriatrics, psychology, physiotherapy, etc. In the past, the need to have staff trained was not as paramount as it is today. In earlier days, our main focus seemed to be primarily custodial in nature. In the late sixties and early seventies, it seemed that our priority was to keep our residents dry, dressed and up. We measured the effectiveness of our care by the number of bedsores our residents "didn't have." Many of those bed sores were "holes to the bone." Now we are hard pressed to find reddened areas let alone bedsores.

Today's mandate of quality of life cannot be easily defined or measured. In the "old days" we need only list for our staff their duties for each shift - who to toilet, bath, feed, dress, etc. Now we go far beyond that. Our staff are now asked to do a more complex task with a more complex resident than what can be defined on any list or schedule. Their role now involves an on-going assessment of the needs of each resident in order to determine what must be done to enhance that person's life. That cannot occur without training.

Without understanding there can be little motivation, little creativity and little self initiative.

When these are lacking, the manager must constantly monitor all of the staff's activities in order to ensure that optimum care is achieved.

IS THE PROBLEM COMMUNICATIONAL?

The effectiveness of any organization depends on the efficiency of its communication network. There are a variety of underlying forces that can discolor how well groups or individuals can relay information accurately. For our discussion, verbal communication will be represented by both spoken and written word. Even though the written word is not expressed directly, its intention is to communicate to individuals when direct contact is not available. Non-verbal communication refers to body language including mannerisms and facial expressions. Hidden communication is interpreting into what is said a different meaning than what was intended.

1) Verbal Communication

A manager in one facility complained "I don't understand it. Nobody seems to follow the instructions I outline in my memos." It is little wonder. Staff called this manager the "Memo King." He would regularly issue numerous memos to be read at the change of shift. The staff frequently heard after report "Don't leave yet, I have some memos I have to read. Memo One . . ., Memo Two . . ., Memo Three . . . " The seventh memo was the most important. By the time it was read, most staff were bored and not listening. In this setting the staff received too much information. They were unable to sort through what was given to determine what was important and what was not. They experienced from management "verbal diarrhea" or information overload.

The other extreme is too little information. When assessing one facility, I asked staff to identify the problems they experienced in their workplace. The first item on the list was "secrets" - no information. In this facility, no one heard anything about anything. When a rumor surfaced "We heard there was going to be lay-off. What do you think?" - managers were instructed to respond "I can't talk about it." That response may suffice if morale is positive and there exists a strong trusting relationship between managers and staff.

When morale is low, the staff will make another assessment. In this facility morale was very shaky. When issues were not discussed, it left staff to determine the truth to the rumor on their own. Their suspicion and mistrust only added credence to what they heard through the staff "grapevine." Needless to say, once the hearsay circulated through the building, the information finally supplied by management took considerable time to correct the falsities generated and belay the suspicions. Even then there were some who would still not believe the truth - "That's not what I heard."

2) Nonverbal Communication

A manager is on display at all times. Frequently it is not what we say but what we do that communicates to staff what we are thinking or how we feel.

In one facility the administrator had a pattern. The only time he was seen on any unit was when there was a problem. Imagine that I am that manager. I walk onto the unit for no specific reason. As soon as staff see me, my presence initiates an immediate response "Oh oh, what's wrong now?" No matter my intentions for being on that unit, it can easily be interpreted differently from their previous experiences.

Take this one step further. Imagine that I am a "dramatist" - no matter what I do, think or say, it is always communicated with exaggerated movements and expressions. I walk onto the unit. Staff are sitting at the desk charting. My presence already creates the belief that there is a problem. I do not say a word to anyone. I stand there for a moment, take a form from the top of the desk, frown and say under my breath "I don't believe this" and walk away. The immediate response after I leave - "We are in for it now!"

In this setting, staff were always left to decide for themselves what is going through their manager's mind. His nonverbal communication was so blatant and his verbal communication so limited, their assumptions always had a negative connotation. They did not look for any other reason and did not believe that they had the freedom to ask him to explain what bothered him. The actual fact in this example is that the manager's behavior may have simply been an uncomfortable bout of "gas."

How staff interpret what they see is based on what has existed in their relationship with management in the past. If that relationship is positive, then their interpretation will be open minded. If the relationship is strained, then their analysis will be guarded. We will expand on this area when we discuss "The Mask of Management."

3) Hidden

There are some staff who are determined to prove their point of view. You send a memo to staff regarding a concern you have. You spend considerable time drafting the contents of that memo and believe it conveys a positive message. The memo is read to staff during report. At the end of report, one staff member with an "ax to grind" takes a couple of others aside and says "Did you hear that memo? You know that's not what they are really saying. If you look between lines three and four, you will know exactly what they mean." This individual is constantly looking for the hidden information and will often find it whether it is there or not.

Communication is a complex process. Without clearly defined mechanisms within an organization to deal with miscommunication and misconceptions, we have the potential of fueling the fires of distrust and misunderstandings.

IS THE PROBLEM INTERPERSONAL?

Any organization is comprised of an assortment of relationships. The perception of managers and staff towards each other can dictate the effectiveness of the interplay between these groups. The more formal and structured the association, the more distant the relationship. Yet a *laissez faire* attitude towards professionalism can allow personality conflicts to govern organizational effectiveness.

1) Personality Conflicts

As we examine the three descriptive styles of managers and the three performance characteristics of staff, we will identify fertile ground for personality conflicts that have the potential of disrupting the smooth progression of the organization. The variety of people with different backgrounds, points of view, needs and belief systems within our facilities creates the potential for conflicts. Left unchecked, these conflicts can disrupt team cooperation and effectiveness. Unless there exists a mechanism that unveils these hidden problems, they cannot be resolved.

2) Professional Conflicts

Direct line staff not only influence the quality of care received, but they also represent that care within the community. Professionalism is essential in our industry regardless of a person's educational level. If all direct line staff, including nursing, housekeeping, dietary and maintenance staff are not considered as "professionals" then professionalism is not expected nor heeded. Without an expectation of professionalism by all staff, the manager finds himself being unjustly challenged by people from the community on what is done or supposedly done within the facility.

Instead of establishing and enforcing a code of conduct for all staff, some organizations resolve their problems with confidentiality in a very peculiar manner. They establish a policy that only allows the registered nurses and other "professionals" to attend care conferences and/or have access to the resident's charts. Direct line staff in these settings are restricted from any information on the resident's chart or are omitted from direct involvement in the development of the resident care plan.

Rather than teaching and enforcing professional conduct, the symptom of the problem is smoothed over by not giving any information to staff. Such professional conflict creates a very delineated atmosphere. Instead of a team environment, two groups emerge - the "professionals" and those who are not. This perception fuels the belief by some direct line staff that they are only good "from the neck down" - their main function is only as technicians, not caregivers.

IS THE PROBLEM PERSONAL?

A person's personality qualities influences how well she can manage. Confidence, mannerisms, skills, analytical abilities, common sense, personality, self-image, etc., all play a role in determining one's effectiveness.

1) Personality Make-Up

There are some who have to work harder than others to be effective managers simply because their own personality characteristics or mannerisms impede their abilities. Imagine that I am your new boss. On first contact I greet you in a very loud and raspy voice "HOW ARE YOU? GOOD, I'M GLAD TO HEAR IT. THANKS FOR JOINING US."

Those who have taken the time to know me have learned that this is how I talk to everyone. They have gone beyond the initial barrier to find that I am easy to get along with and easy going. Unfortunately, many decided on my personal qualities by how I talk to them. They avoid me because they are either afraid or uncomfortable with my rough and aggressive manner. A manager with an intimidating demeanor must constantly compensate for his mannerism and voice tones.

The fear of talking in front of a group is another example of how one's personality make-up can influence his ability as an effective manager. Any manager who has this difficulty finds it impossible to resolve organizational problems if he cannot be involved in the discussion. When staff identify a problem that requires discussion at the next management meeting, this manager will find that his fear results in a poor presentation of the problem, jeopardizing its successful resolution. What staff encounter is an inability to solve problems, not because the problem is insurmountable, but because the manager they must deal with cannot function well within a group.

2) Hidden Agendas

You are my "boss." I have had three other "bosses" before. In each case all three were ineffective and couldn't be trusted. It is not surprising that my immediate perception of you is the same. If I was "burned" by the last three, I will probably not risk letting it happen with you. My hidden agenda is simple - I believe I know you and what you do, not by who you are, but by your title.

There can be nothing more challenging than replacing an ineffective, incompetent manager. Some staff have the potential of interpreting your actions and behavior based on their previous experiences with that past manager. This influences their second guessing the motives behind your every move. In such a setting, your actions to encourage staff to be open and discuss their problems may only be met with suspicion and a guarded response.

3) Internal/External/Assertive

An "internal" manager is a person who is shy and mild mannered - one who does not deal well with conflict or aggressive outbursts and has difficulty defending controversial issues. In one facility my contact with the director of resident care immediately raised a red flag. I wanted to test my suspicions. I asked for a meeting with the director of resident care and her registered nursing staff. I began the meeting and directed the group through a problem solving discussion where I recorded their comments on a flip chart. The nurses around the table were actively involved in the process and worked through the issues objectively and thoroughly. After ten minutes, I sat down and asked the director of care to take over.

This manager was a timid lady who had difficulty being assertive. My original suspicion was that she had problems controlling a group. When she took over the group discussion, she began in a very soft and mild voice. She asked those sitting at the table "What else would you like to add?" The group process soon disintegrated. Before long two nurses at one end of the table began talking to each other. Then two more started a separate conversation at the other side of the table. All of this occurring while their manager was trying to complete the task at hand. Eventually the group lost its direction.

This manager needed to compensate for her timid personality by learning how to assert herself. Without those skills, her other strengths as a manager were easily eradicated.

An "external" manager is one who is always outspoken, often appearing aggressive in nature. This type of person challenges everything and anything. Another appropriate term for this personality quality is the "crusader" - an individual who finds a cause in everything, never letting anything go by without a fight.

The crusader is quickly identified by others in the organization. The agenda during every meeting the crusader attends seems to be read in the following manner:

> "Item #1 . . . Donna (the crusader) what do you have to say?"
> "Item #2 . . . Donna what do you have to say?"
> "Item #3 . . . Donna what do you have to say?"

Everyone becomes so familiar with the crusader's challenges, they are able to predict her responses.

A crusader soon becomes harried. When everyone can predict your pattern, they can learn how to defuse you. They move their focus from the issue to challenging the crusader. Their defense is based on what the crusader will probably say. The crusader soon finds that things become more difficult to resolve. Before each meeting she will only know what is on the agenda. When an issue arises and the crusader begins to make her comments or raises her objections, someone else will immediately respond - "I have information that supports what I am saying." The crusader is unprepared and cannot make a strong enough rebuttal. With the challenges being prepared in advance, the effectiveness of the crusader is soon lost.

The "assertive" manager is one who has the ability to draw others up to their full potential; the sensitivity to adjust her approach as the need arises; the conviction to defend issues she sees important; the insight to identify her own strength and limitations; and the common sense to utilize her energy and resources to their fullest. These are the qualities of the Effective Manager that will be expanded as the following chapters unfold.

SUMMARY - WHERE IS THE PROBLEM?

The challenge in managing is determining the problem. It would be easy if management were only a style or technique. We could then ensure that proficiency in that technique would allow us to be effective in every setting. It is not so simple. To be effective in leading others, a manager must assume a certain responsibility. That responsibility involves acquiring the necessary knowledge and skills that will develop effective interpersonal and personal abilities. Once these abilities are acquired, then and only then can she have the insight to define the problem and decide how to resolve it.

The role of "manager" is an extensive and far reaching one. Its complexities and challenges become the foundation from which the organization is built.

The plot thickens.

Chapter Three

LONG TERM CARE
THE NATURE OF THE BEAST

PART ONE: INTERDEPARTMENTAL RELATIONSHIPS

What would happen if nursing staff were thirty minutes late getting the residents to breakfast?

What would happen if dietary were thirty minutes late getting breakfast ready?

The ramifications of these two scenarios are clearly evident to those working in our setting. Ours is a tightly interwoven organization. What occurs in one department has dramatic effects on another. To you, that may not be surprising, but when you compare it with other organizations and the ramifications they would experience, it demonstrates a significant differences.

Most organizations are horizontal in nature (*figure #6*). Even though departments may be interrelated, they are not interdependent. In the production of a car, the construction of each component of a car is a separate process with little dependency on other departments. One team builds carburetors, another builds chassis, another tires, and still another assembles all of the parts to make the vehicle. If there is a problem in constructing carburetors, the other departments can keep working, having no influence on how well the tires or chassis are built. The worst thing that can happen is the line shuts down and production is halted when existing inventory of that part has been exhausted. The factory will not produce the same number of cars, but what they do produce is *still a car*. Even if one component of the car is constructed poorly and doesn't work properly, the end product is *still a car*. It doesn't run, but it is a car.

In fact when a specific problem is identified, it can often wait until the car is built and off the assembly line, where a special team will isolate that car and correct the defective part before it is shipped.

(Figure #6)

In this type of organization the product is at the end of the process. Each department stands on its own, effected only indirectly by the problems or difficulties of the other departments.

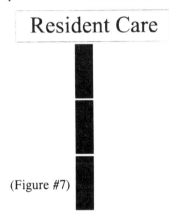

Resident Care

(Figure #7)

Our organization can appropriately be called vertical (*Figure #7*). Each department is balanced by the other, keeping our product - Resident Care - in proper position.

To demonstrate the significance of interdepartmental relationships in our specialty, let us examine the ramifications of a late breakfast. What would be the impact if the residents were to arrive to the dining room thirty minutes late?

When one department falls behind, the whole organization is effected. Being late for a meal does not only create problems for dietary, but it impacts on recreation, housekeeping and all other departments as well. More importantly our product (resident care) is significantly impacted. Not only is nursing criticized for not getting the residents to the dining room on time, dietary will also hear from the residents "My breakfast is cold." Something they had no control over. The dietary department is now scurrying trying to get back on schedule in order to be ready for lunch.

Likewise, the residents are returning to the unit at 0930 instead of 0900 hours. That half hour now interferes with the recreation staff.

Programs normally scheduled for 0900 hours have to be canceled or the whole schedule for that day restructured. The complaint from the residents "I always go to crafts at 0900, why do you have to cancel that program?" When something happens to one department, it will dramatically effect our end product (resident care).

A factory does not experience this intensity of interdependence. When the carburetor is constructed poorly, no one complains of the paint job or how the doors are installed. In our setting, any problem in one department will tilt the column and influence all others (*Figure #8*).

(Figure #8)

Shift the problem slightly. Instead of breakfast at the usual time of 0800 hours, it is not ready until 0830 hours. How does that effect nursing or recreation and more importantly resident care?

In long term care, we are highly dependent on each other in order to complete our job. Everything we do sends ripples throughout the organization effecting all of its components.

In long term care we have interdependence without commonalty. Nursing, dietary and recreation are as different as tires are to carburetors. This creates the potential for significant conflicts in interdepartmental relationships. The ensuing frustrations are due to the dissimilarities of each department in their focus and priority. We can best demonstrate these potential interdepartmental conflicts by comparing only two departments - nursing and dietary.

1) Shifts

Dietary	Nursing
0600 - 1400 hours	0730 - 1500 hours
1100 - 1900 hours	1500 - 2330 hours
0800 - 1600 hours	2330 - 0700 hours

Shifts in the dietary department generally overlap, covering approximately sixteen hours of each day. Shifts in the nursing department are separate, covering twenty four hours of each day. This creates a significant difference in departmental communications. The following example demonstrates the impact of this difference.

The director of resident care and director of dietary attend a department head meeting. They are required to inform their staff about a new policy being implemented. If both department heads *work 0800 to 1600 hours*, can each notify the majority of their staff directly about that policy? The director of dietary probably can. She will have some exceptions. A few of her staff may be off duty that day. Likewise, she may not see a couple of casual staff or students working later in the evening shift to help with dishes. Generally she will be able to make direct contact with the majority of her staff in a one day period.

The director of resident care on the other hand has a greater challenge. Depending on the size of the facility and the number of units, it is almost impossible for her to make direct contact with the majority of her staff. If there are three units, it is a complex task to meet all staff on all units as they are coming and going at the change of shift. She will also miss a number of staff who are off duty and a significant number of part time and casual staff as well.

The director of resident care must rely on her charge nurses or unit managers to pass on the information. The first and most obvious problem is that the unit managers are relaying second-hand information. They were not at the meeting when the policy was discussed. Instead, they are sharing with their staff what they believe their manager said was important about that policy. In the dietary department, most staff receive first-hand information from their department head.

It does not end there. The unit manager who received the information from the director of resident care must then pass the information to the manager on the next shift. She passes the information to staff working the afternoon shift and also to the unit manager working on the night shift. That manager relays the information to her staff and the part time manager the next day, who passes it to those staff who were not on the day before and on and on it goes. In the nursing department, the information passes through so many hands that it is little wonder it becomes distorted and diluted. At the next department head meeting the nursing department is questioned why the policy is not completely implemented, when the other departments were able to do it so quickly.

Communication in the dietary department from manager to staff is *direct*. The department head has the opportunity to relay information and resolve problems face-to-face with all staff. In the nursing department communication is *indirect*. Information and problem solving must rely on a number of different managers (both full and part time) who themselves do not have frequent direct contact with their department head.

When departments do not understand each other, a common criticism can be heard - "Doesn't nursing staff talk to each other? All of the other departments know what is going on!"

2) Tasks

In the dietary department, the cook knows what he has to do at 1000 hours each morning. In fact in a well run dietary department all staff know what they are suppose to be doing almost every minute of the day. An efficient dietary department is like a well oiled machine.. It is a highly structured department that provides very little flexibility for any of its staff to diverge from the set routine.

In nursing it is another story. A staff member performing care in a resident's room at 0845 hours this morning, cannot be guaranteed she will be in that same room, doing the same thing, tomorrow morning at that time. No matter how much energy is invested to structure nursing schedules and routines, it will never completely materialize. Our job is sporadic - totally dictated by the need at that time. In fact if necessary, the entire nursing department could virtually stop everything for an hour to deal with a crisis. If dietary were to stop everything for an hour, it would be a crisis.

These are important dynamics that can create significant interdepartmental conflicts. Nursing staff have the opportunity to be more flexible in their routine than dietary staff. Nursing could schedule a care conference at 1100 hours, but dietary staff would be unable to attend. Eleven in the morning is an hour before lunch, one of the busiest times of the day.

Nursing could even push tasks into tomorrow if necessary. This can be easily demonstrated. Imagine the impact if the water supply were shut off in the building today. It would be difficult, but nursing could still function. Baths would be re-scheduled throughout the rest of the week. When the water is off for the day, dietary would be devastated.

These subtle differences can create common complaints of one department towards another. Nursing staff can lament -

"Why can't dietary staff be more flexible? All we are asking them
    to do is attend a twenty minute impromptu care conference."
"We just want them to have a meal later."
"We just want them to start breakfast on a different unit."
"We just want them to . . ."

Their lack of understanding of how the dietary department runs can result in undue frustration and conflict when that department does not appear as flexible. Likewise the dietary staff can be just as critical - "All we ask nursing to do is have the residents to the dining room on time. It's a simple request." What they may not realize is that seven residents experienced diarrhea ten minutes before breakfast.

3) Peak Demand

The peak demand time is the time period where staff are encountering the greatest work load. In nursing, that demand varies from shift to shift (*figure #9*). During the day shift, the peak demand is usually between 0730 to 1230 hours. As the shift progresses, the demand diminishes. By the end of the shift (1400 to 1500 hours) the unit can be fairly quiet. Of course there are exceptions to this pattern - *some* shifts are hectic for the entire eight hours and others are slow from beginning to end.

During the afternoon shift, the nursing peak demand is usually a half hour before supper until 2130 hours. The beginning and end of the shift is generally quiet, barring any unforeseen disruptions. During the night shift the peak demand is from 0430 hours until shift end at 0700 hours, with the beginning of the shift generally being very quiet.

(Figure #9)

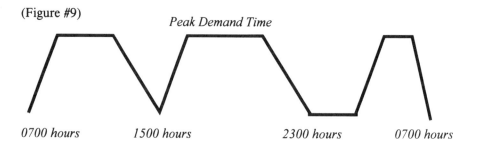

Peak Demand Time

0700 hours   *1500 hours*   *2300 hours*   *0700 hours*

The peak demand times for dietary are quite straightforward - breakfast, lunch and supper (*figure #10*). The period before a meal is the most hectic. The closer to mealtime, the crazier the department can be in attempting to get everything ready. As soon as the meal is over the pace comes to a near halt. In fact in the dietary departments, many staff probably have their coffee break right after the residents have their meal. They know that it is too early to prepare for the next meal. All that is needed now is to clean up from the last one. Taking a break any later would be at a time when they are doing most of the preparation for the next meal.

(Figure #10)   *Peak Demand Time*

0800 hours   *1200 hours*   *1700 hours*

These patterns can create a significant perceptual conflict between departments. When dietary staff walk past the nursing station at 1430 hours and find nursing staff sitting at the desk, their immediate thought can be - "I keep hearing nursing needs more staff. Every time I walk past the desk they are just sitting there doing nothing but writing in the chart." Conversely, nursing staff can see dietary staff having a cup of coffee at 0900 hours, and their thought - "It must be nice!" No wonder problems with departmental harmony erupt. When staff do not understand a department's peak times, they cannot relate to what is occurring.

These departmental misconceptions are most evident when a staff member transfers from one department to another. After a short time that person will virtually undergo a cultural shock, being heard to say "I never knew you were that busy."

LOOKING FOR ISLANDS

It is important to define the interdepartmental relations within an organization. These relationships have a significant impact on team effectiveness, communication and problem solving. When staff and managers believe there is little commonality between departments in their needs, experiences and abilities, there can develop:

islands - isolating of one department from another.

These islands can best be seen in the dining room during staff coffee break - nursing staff are at one table, housekeeping at another, dietary at another, management possibly at another.

In one large facility it was easy to demonstrate how entrenched these islands can be. Managers of that organization were asked to meet in the dining room five minutes before staff were to arrive for break. A manager was placed at each table. Nine housekeeping staff walked through the dining room door. They froze when they noticed that a manager was at each table. They looked at each other. One turned and said to the group "There is no place to sit." Unfortunately a two foot by two foot table in the corner of the room was missed. No manager was sitting at that table. Needless to say, all nine housekeepers surrounded it for the entire break. How the housekeepers responded was highly reflective of the dynamics and friction that existed within that facility.

TRANSCENDING DEPARTMENTAL BOUNDARIES

In long term care, we are required to work together but we are always in potential conflict. Departmental relationships can be in constant discord in *competing for resources*, transcending *lines of authority* and disputing over *degree of involvement..*

COMPETITION FOR RESOURCES

Each facility has *limited* resources in money, equipment, staffing hours and space. All departments within the facility usually require more of each of these and the staff of each department believe that their needs have the greater priority. These limited resources can create competition, and the staff's perception create a win/lose outcome.

If the capital expenditure for equipment purchases this year was $10,000, and both dietary and nursing requested equipment worth that amount, who gets it? Nursing staff have asked for a powered lift to assist them with the increase in heavy care residents. The dietary staff have stated that an outdated and unreliable steam cooker needs replacing because it is not performing the job well enough. Whoever gets what they need sets in motion a potential conflict. Criticism by the staff of one department that the other is being favored, that their role and needs are not respected, that they are not as important as the other, etc., sets the framework for interdepartmental jealousy and strained relations.

TRANSCENDING LINES OF AUTHORITY

Most organizational charts show specific lines of authority - the director of resident care and director of dietary are at an equal level of authority, with their staff reporting to them. That delineation does not accurately describe the functional lines of authority that occur in the day-to-day operation. When the director of dietary sees nursing staff doing something that jeopardizes the well being or safety of a resident, she cannot ignore it. When the director of resident care sees a dietary staff member doing something inappropriate, she as well must take action. Likewise, the unit manager must ensure consistency regardless of the department involved.

In long term care we have organizational charts within organizational charts with no clear boundaries. The unit manager often has an informal line of communication and authority with the dietary department in the day-to-day operations of her unit, showing a lateral reporting and authority process. Likewise, the unit manager generally has the freedom to order supplies from the kitchen, deal with special concerns of each resident, adjust routines where required, etc. without the constant need of going through the department heads. The management of resident care transcends all departmental boundaries.

No other organization has such complex inter-workings as long term care. In industry, the organizational chart is clearly defined and strictly followed. The chain of command usually defines that the plant supervisor manages the building, his foremen report to him and his staff to the foreman. The director of sales would never think of stopping a man on the assembly line to correct him in what he is doing. He would present it to the plant supervisor who would direct his staff accordingly.

Long term care's uniqueness is that all staff of every department have direct contact with resident care. That surpasses the formal boundaries normally encountered in a manager's role. When we manage, we manage an organization not a department. No matter what the managers title, the role is broad in its spectrum. Unfortunately, when that role is not clearly defined, staff corrected by the manager of another department can comment - "She is not my boss" or "I don't have to listen to her."

DEGREE OF INVOLVEMENT

Some of the most influential staff in resident care are housekeepers. In certain situations, they have more rapport with specific residents than other staff.

Imagine you are a seventy-eight year old resident. As a lay person, your only contact with long term care was through admission. Your

49

knowledge of the specialty and the organization is minimal. Let us examine your potential relationship with nursing and housekeeping.

Could you relate to the roll and responsibilities of the nurse on duty? You may be familiar with what she does for you, but you will probably have little insight into her involvement with the other thirty-nine residents on your unit.

What about your understanding of the housekeeper's role and duties? She is doing something that you have probably done most of your life - clean. You can immediately relate to her, feeling that the two of you have much in common.

If a nurse were in your room yesterday morning at 0915 hours, does it mean that she will be in your room this morning at 0915 hours? Highly unlikely! Nursing staff often rotate shifts. You can't even be guaranteed to see the same nurse the next day let alone spend the same time with her.

If a housekeeper cleaned your room yesterday morning at 0915 hours, the chances are she will be doing that at the same time every morning. A housekeeper's role is more structured and the staff more consistent in their assignment. As a resident, you will probably see the same housekeeper, the same time each day, further enhancing your relationship with her.

Finally, the nurse can be somewhat demanding. Always asking you to do things that are threatening and uncomfortable. - such as walking, bathing, eating, exercising, etc.

On the other hand, the appearance of the housekeeper can be less stressful. She places few demands on you.

The frequency of contact and the intensity of the relationship between the resident and the housekeeper can be a valuable asset to the care team. It is the housekeeper who may know the most about certain aspects of a specific resident and may provide insight into understanding that person's needs and actions.

No other setting has more of a need than long term care to integrated its departments. Most hospitals do not include the housekeeping or maintenance staff in a care conferences. Their involvement is not seen as crucial to the outcome of the expected care process. In long term care it is essential that we transcend all barriers to meld together into one homogeneous group in order to be effective. This need places an added responsibility on every manager within the facility, whether administrator, department head or unit manager.

Part Two: PROBLEM MANAGERS AND MANAGEMENT DYNAMICS

It is important at this point to discuss how a manager's style can enhance or hinder the positive dynamics within an organization. Again I must restate both the limitation and the caution identified at the beginning of the text. What is presented in the following pages is a general description of three management styles - the EFFECTIVE MANAGER, the manager who MUST MANAGE, and the manager who IS MANAGED. These categories do not describe the total depth of a manager's ability, nor do they imply that all managers must fit strictly in one grouping or the other. The intention is to create a general portrayal that will demonstrate the effects of certain qualities on the overall operation of the facility.

The caution is straightforward - do not jump to conclusions. We will discuss all levels of management from the poor administrator, to a poorly functioning board, to an incompetent director of resident care, to an ineffective unit manager. No one position is the root of the problem and no one position is the only source for the solution.

Remember that the play is continuing to unfold. You will now be led to a few of the possible "who done its" mentioned in chapter one. There are solutions to the dynamics described in the following pages. You will learn not only how to manage your staff more effectively, but also how to manage your manager as well. Let the play take its course. It has a positive ending.

THE EFFECTIVE MANAGER

The EFFECTIVE MANAGER is an individual who maintains a very strict philosophy - "*I hired you to do a job, therefore go and do it.*" It is her belief that most of her staff are competent individuals who have the desire to perform their job to the best of their ability. This manager is open minded and approachable, encouraging those under her charge to discuss any issue that effects their performance. She is able to promote and utilize a team approach in problem solving, but has no difficulty making decisions or challenging poor performance or work attitudes. As a manager, this person is an effective motivator who has the ability to keep the organization, department or unit running smoothly. Through her management style, she has the ability to assist others to function at their maximum level, clearly defining goals, and setting realistic expectations for performance.

This person does not have to be liked, but does not go out of her way to be disliked. She knows that there is never a decision that can be made that will please everyone. She involves her staff in participatory management. When a decision must be made, her staff are part of the process. They are encouraged to recommend what they believe would be the best course of action. Invariably there will be disagreements among staff on the direction to take. Some will want to go one way and the rest another. This manager knows that no matter what decision is made, someone will not be pleased. Decisions are made on what seems to be the best direction to take at the time. She focuses and emphasizes to others the importance of outcome (what we want to achieve), as well as process (how it is done).

The EFFECTIVE MANAGER is open minded and flexible. She encourages staff to continually evaluate what is being done and communicate their findings, whether positive or negative. If necessary, decisions will be adjusted based on the results of their evaluation. Even though some staff may strongly disagree with the direction taken, they cannot deny that this manager is generally fair, open minded and approachable. She may not be liked by all, but she is respected.

The EFFECTIVE MANAGER has a further quality. This person does not need to "carry a big stick," but everyone knows that she has one. When an incident occurs that requires correction, this manager would rather counsel staff initially than jump to reprimand or criticize. Her management philosophy is to bring the best out of her staff. She will give a staff member the benefit of the doubt when most incidents occur, and work with that person to help correct the problem identified.

If that same incident should occur again, this manager will take the necessary steps to resolve it. She will establish with the employee clearly defined performance expectations that are achievable and measurable. The staff member in question is always aware of the consequences should those goals not be met in the specified time frame. This manager ensures that every step is taken to help this person meet those goals (further education, establishing specific schedules, hands on teaching, referral to available counseling services, etc.).

Should the same incident occur again, the first step of the reprimand process will begin - a verbal warning. This manager will still work with the employee to correct the problem. If the incident occurs again, the reprimand will then go to the next stage - a written warning, and all the way to dismissal if necessary.

In many cases this manager will not need to fire an employee. This process of defining the required performance standards, assisting the staff member to meet them and explaining the consequences, will usually end in a *win/win* situation. Either the staff member will learn how to meet the expectations or will be so conscious of the ultimate decision, he/she will resign rather than wait to be fired.

There is no question that the EFFECTIVE MANAGER is a risk taker. She knows that growth means that things will not always go the way planned. When something goes wrong, it becomes a learning experience to determine the required solution to take the next step successfully.

This is an effective leader, keeping staff excited, providing a working environment that recognizes and taps their strengths, striving to ensure that they have the tools, supports and resources to allow them to do their job to the best of their ability. This manager knows that she is successful when she asks staff how things are after being away for a few days, and they respond "Have you been away?" This demonstrates that her staff are functioning well as a team, able to work on their own without their manager having to be present all of the time. Her staff have shown that they are self motivated and self-managed.

THOSE WHO MUST MANAGE

There was an article written called "The Fallacy of the One Big Brain." How appropriate! The manager who MUST MANAGE believes that he knows everyone's job better than the person who is assigned to do it. He frequently demonstrates a lack of faith in trusting the insights and abilities of others.

In one organization the director of resident care so strongly believed that no one could make decisions effectively without her input, that she required the unit managers to call her day or night for permission to go into the store room to get more supplies. You can imagine the number of calls she received. In another organization the administrator would not let anyone in the facility to open the mail (other than resident mail), whether it was addressed to their department or not. He set a policy that all mail was to be sent to his office and then he would forward it to the appropriate department if he felt it was worthwhile. There was a feeling on his part that his managers and staff couldn't be trusted to know what to do with it without his input.

Such a manager has a tremendous need to be in control. This person will dominate an organization, department or unit, stifling any active, sincere problem solving. He may go through the motions of listening to others, but he does not hear them. He has already decided what is wrong and how it will be resolved before his staff become involved.

I can often identify this manager at seminars. He always has a beeper. I am not suggesting that every manager with a beeper is this person. If the manager is on call, then it is understandable that he would have a beeper in case there is an emergency. The manager who MUST MANAGE not only has the beeper at the session, but it is going off constantly, requiring him to jump up to the phone repeatedly throughout the day. This demonstrates that his staff are not allowed to make decisions without checking with him first.

Imagine that you are the director of resident care, an EFFECTIVE MANAGER, and I am the administrator, a manager who MUST MANAGE. You have worked with your unit managers (also EFFECTIVE MANAGERS) on a problem within your department and identified a solution to resolve that problem. You know that in this organization you cannot implement anything without approval by the "boss." You share with me the direction you intend to take. (By the way, this manager is always addressed "Mr.," "Mrs.," or "Miss" _____, never by his/her first name. There is little informality with this type of manager).

My immediate response to your proposal is - "That is not the direction I want this organization to take. This is what I want you to do." No matter how much you attempt to promote your case, the manager who MUST MANAGE will simply "put his foot down." You return to your unit managers and state "The Administrator does not agree with the direction we were going to take. He wants us to do the following . . ." You now outline something that you and the unit managers know is not applicable to what is occurring in the department and will be difficult to implement. What is their response? They are deflated, confused and frustrated. Who do they blame? They may blame the administrator, but rarely does anyone only blame the person two levels up. They will probably place some of the blame on you, believing that you could have backed them on this one if you really tried.

It is not surprising that many in this organization will learn that it is easier and quicker with such a "boss" to just bring him the information and wait for him to tell you what he wants done. Staff begin to believe that they are not trusted, deciding that their role is not to think but just to do. In fact in some organizations the staff under this manager's rule view their importance "from the neck down" only.

The manager who MUST MANAGE always complains - "I am so busy," and so he is. This person ends up doing everybody else's job. In such a setting, managers can find themselves in an awkward situation if they attempt to do anything without his knowledge and approval. The manager who MUST MANAGE will undoubtedly run into problems as time passes. He will find that he cannot keep up with the demands on his time. This manager continually needs to be in seven places at one time. Everyone waits for him to tell them what he wants done now. Creating this type of control results in the organization eventually sliding in its effectiveness. He will not be able to meet the demand. As things start to fall apart, it only reinforces his belief that people cannot be trusted to do their jobs without his having to watch over them constantly. He will only tighten the screws a bit more to try and compensate. The cycle accelerates.

This type of manager has one other destructive quality. He is a person who must be in the forefront at all times. One executive director with this management style presented at a convention on something implemented in his organization. All one had to do was count the number of times he said "I" in his presentation - "*I* did . . ., *I* implemented . . ., etc." He was never heard to say "My staff . . ." or "Our organization . . ." One wonders that if this type of manager did not get his picture in the local newspaper weekly, he would inevitably go through some type of withdrawal. His need to be in the forefront seems paramount. In fact an executive director in one organization would not allow anyone to write and submit an article for publication unless his name was on that article. His belief was that nothing happened in the organization without him, therefore he also deserved the credit for success. Needless to say, no one in the organization submitted any publications.

Staff soon learn that the only way to get around this restrictive problem solving process is by:

"PLANTING THE SEED"

Informally talking to the boss about an idea. They need only wait for a period of time after the seed is planted to find that this manager will present the idea as his own. It is no wonder that under this style, people not only stop thinking, they also stop being creative. Why do anything when everything you do is taken over as his?

This person rules by an "iron fist in a velvet glove." To those outside the organization (or unit as we will soon discover), he seems to run a smooth ship. To those working under this manager, it is a tight ship with little opportunity for individuality except for the boss.

THE MANAGER WHO IS MANAGED

This is a person who does not have the management skills to perform the job, which results in his being afraid of conflict of any type. This style places an organization, department or unit into a state of apathy.

When assessing a facility, I will ask casual staff what must seem as a peculiar question - "Can you tell me what your administrator looks like?" I have found that some staff will respond "I don't really know." A manager who IS MANAGED becomes so uncomfortable with the demands of the job that he actually hides. His day, every day, starts and ends at the same time, always having lunch from 1200 to 1300 hours. This punctuality is not an indication of his effectiveness, but of his avoidance.

Whether it is an administrator or director of resident care, you will find this person in his office or if a unit manager, in the medication room or behind the desk. This is a "bottom line manager" -

⇒ for an administrator his main occupation is to ensure the budget is on target.
⇒ for a director of resident care she concentrates her efforts on reports, staff scheduling and paper work.
⇒ for a unit manager the emphasis is on charting, medication and the completion of physical care (all of the baths and beds are done).

These are non-threatening issues. The people issues involving residents, family or staff are another matter.

You will have difficulty finding the manager who IS MANAGED at a long term care convention. He will have gone to the convention, but rarely take part in any of the educational sessions. If he has to make an appearance, he will usually stand at the back (this does not imply that everyone standing at the back is this type of manager). When he is required to talk with other professionals about "quality of life" and "quality of care" he uses all the catch phrases of the time, but hasn't the slightest idea what they mean or how to implement them.

The manager who IS MANAGED is managed by conflict. Imagine that the administrator of your organization had this management style. You are the director of resident care and an EFFECTIVE MANAGER. You enter his office (by the way this type of manager is always addressed by everyone by his first name) and ask "Is it all right if I implement a new program called X?"

Have you seen those little toy dogs in the back of car windows whose head bobs up and down as the car moves? That is this manager. His immediate response to almost every and all requests is "OK" (possibly with his head bobbing up and down at the same time).

His style also employs one other survival strategy - nothing is ever in writing or if it is documented, it is very vague. The very next day another department head enters his office and asks if she can do "Y" - the complete opposite to "X." His response - "OK" (head bobbing up and down). Again nothing is in writing. With this manager, there is no well defined or even consistent direction. Everyone seems to be going in every direction all at the same time, usually accomplishing very little. It is obvious that this manager creates chaos within the organization.

Let us take this further. Three months after permission was received to implement 'X,' you return to my office stating "I have experienced a problem with the union about 'X' and I need your support." His response "You have a problem with what?" Your answer "The program 'X' you told me three months ago I could do." "I don't remember telling you anything about a program 'X' (remember when nothing is in writing, it allows for selective memory loss). Tell me what that was." You outline the program as you did three months ago. His response "That's not what I thought you were going to do." You get no support and are held accountable for any fallout that may occur.

The survival skill of this management style is to *delegate blame* - the ability to deflect responsibility for any mistakes or failures onto others is the key to his possible longevity as a manager. When nothing is in writing, it becomes your word against his and as your boss, his word has more clout. You may attempt to rectify that problem by documenting discussions and sending him a copy, but he rarely responds, or when he does, it is usually vague, making no commitment. In either case no one ever receives a formal "OK" to anything. This allows this manager to reverse his decision when things become uncomfortable.

Bizarre management problems occur when any setting is governed by conflict. One of your staff asks you for a day off. You tell her she cannot have it. Your rationale is legitimate. You either cannot afford to let any one off at that time due to a staff shortage or her sick time is so high she doesn't merit it. Therefore, your answer to her is "no."

Staff in this type of organization soon learn that when they do not get the answer they want from you, they simply bypass you and go directly to the administrator. That staff member asks the administrator "Can I have some extra time off?" His answer - "OK"(head bobbing). She then returns to you saying "The administrator said I could have the time off." You confront him in his office (where you will always find him), "Why did you tell that staff member she could have the time off when I told her she couldn't?"

Now the administrator has a problem. He has to weigh where the greatest degree of conflict lies - does he lose more by telling a unionized employee that she cannot do what he said she could or by telling the *one* director of resident care who is *under his authority* to give her the time off. "Give her the time off." You soon find that your authority is watered down as staff learn that they can override any ruling you make by simply pressuring the administrator.

Take this even further. One of your unit managers reprimands a staff member for inappropriate conduct. That manager presents to you the reasons for the reprimand and how it was conducted. You agree with her actions and support her on her decision. By this time, you have probably learned that you must get the administrator's "OK" before anyone else does. You approach him in his office - "One of my unit managers reprimanded a staff member. I backed her decision, you agree don't you?" His response - "OK" (head bobbing).

Unfortunately that safeguard may not be sufficient. In this organization there exists the ultimate conflict - a union grievance. Some staff learn that when anything is submitted as a grievance level, this administrator will always back down. Organizations such as this have a pattern of never challenging a union grievance regardless of the issue or circumstances involved. This type of manager always gives the same reasons - "It is not worth the fight," "It is too costly," "We won't win anyway."

Once a grievance on the reprimand is received, the administrator tells you that it must be withdrawn. How does his decision influence the unit manager's perception of you? In her eyes, you let her down.

Again, it is the most immediate manager staff hold partially accountable, not just the manager two levels higher. You accomplish other things that seem even more difficult, but instead you gave in. There is a belief that you could have stood your ground if you wanted.

No one understands your job but you. You know that there was no way to convince the administrator to fight the grievance, so you were forced to back away from it. How quickly will your unit manager reprimand another staff member in the future? Most managers in this type of organization become "gun shy," avoiding contentious issues because they will not be supported in their decisions.

The impact of the manager who IS MANAGED is still not complete. Staff or middle managers who want to see things changed usually develop a hidden channel of communication directly to the administrator's "boss" (e.g. the board of directors, owner or executive director). A frustrated staff member will find a board member with a listening ear and talk to him "off the record" about problems in the organization.

At the next board meeting, that board member confronts the administrator - "I heard there is a problem with 'X.' What's going on?" The administrator's response is simple "I'm not aware of there being a problem. I'll check it out and get back to you at the next meeting." Of course nothing is done about it, hoping that it will be forgotten. At the next meeting if the original board member questions the administrator again, he will probably respond "I took care of that problem. I talked to the director of resident care and told her not to do it again." Delegating blame allows anyone to avoid accountability for any actions. Any manager who IS MANAGED can survive a long time in any organization if he can successfully skirt responsibility.

This is still not complete. Some staff learn that the only way to accomplish anything is to just do it and hope it doesn't back fire to become an issue that requires support from upper management. A board member says to this administrator "I hear you have a very good program running on one of your units, glad to hear it." This administrator is hardly on the units and may not know what the board member is talking about. Along with the skill of delegating blame comes a second survival talent - *assigning success* - "Thank you, we worked hard at that and I am pleased that you heard it is working so well."

A vicious circle develops for this manager. The need to avoid conflict initiates an apathy around this manager, which generates a new set of conflicts requiring a more complex survival pattern - delegating blame entwined with assigning success. It is inevitable that this cycle will not only confuse those working in the organization, but exhaust this manager as time passes.

There is an important point being demonstrated with the description of the last two management styles. Personal management skills may not accurately reflect management success. Success in any organization depends as much on the skills of the managers above you, below you or next to you. If you have a "boss" that IS MANAGED or MUST MANAGE, your efforts are dramatically curtailed. No matter what your personal management style, your skills may be diluted when the environment in which you work is not supportive. This is demonstrated by the wheel-barrow imagery in chapter one where the wheel is intact and the person pushing it has the ability to lift it but the load is too heavy.

Your effectiveness as a manager is highly dependent on the environment in which you work. The challenge of the EFFECTIVE MANAGER is to decide - "How do I compensate for an organization that has taught its staff not to think and be creative?" Or "How do I motivate staff who have learned not to take risks?" The actual question is - "How do I manage my manager?" This is part of the intervention strategies discussed in later chapters.

THE MANAGEMENT CONTINUUM

Instead of a clear delineation of three distinct management styles, there really exists a continuum:

$$\longleftarrow \qquad \longrightarrow$$

IS MANAGED------EFFECTIVE MANAGER------MUST MANAGE

Some managers are exactly as we have described the manager who IS MANAGED. On the other hand, some have a few of the skills of an EFFECTIVE MANAGER, but shy away from conflict on certain issues.

Still others are EFFECTIVE MANAGERS in all situations. Others have a few skills of the EFFECTIVE MANAGER but tend to take control under specific circumstances. Others are exactly like the manager who MUST MANAGE.

Defining where one lies on this continuum is the key in determining which skills are needed to be more effective with those under one's charge.

MANAGEMENT DYNAMICS

A problem manager can exist anywhere within an organization. It is time now to expand our investigation beyond the administrator. To do this, we can compare the scope of management influence to a triangle (*figure #11*). The top of the triangle is the board, owner or executive director, next is the administrator, then the department heads, unit managers and then staff. We will look at each of these levels, starting with board.

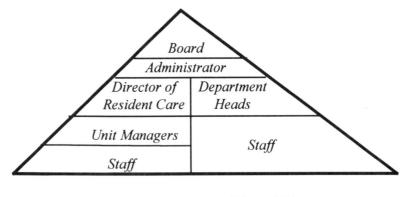

(Figure #11)

THE BOARD (EXECUTIVE DIRECTOR, OWNER)

Management dynamics start at the top with the board. As administrator, you may be a very EFFECTIVE MANAGER. At a department head meeting, your team identifies a problem within the organization and outlines the strategy they believe would be the most effective to resolve it. You take their suggestion to the board for approval. The board consists of EFFECTIVE MANAGERS. Each board member, in order to fulfill their duties effectively, has taken the responsibility to understand the facility and the needs of long term care and its clientele. As they see it, the role of the board is to enhance the problem solving ability of the administrator and provide direction to the organization as a whole. When you present your proposal to this board, they objectively discuss its feasibility. If they believe it is an appropriate course of action, they will support it.

Take that same problem and solution to a board composed of individuals who MUST MANAGE. The results will be dramatically different. Any board, owner or executive director who believes they MUST MANAGE takes control. You present the proposal to this board and their response is simple "This is not the direction we want the organization to go. This is what we think is happening and how we want you to deal with it."

The administrator tells the department heads - "I'm sorry but the board does not agree with our recommendations. They have identified a different course of action." As mentioned earlier, most look at their immediate manager as part of any problem experienced. The department heads can easily question why the administrator backed down. They know that he has convinced the board to support more contentious programs in the past. Most staff and managers within the facility have never dealt with the board directly and are not aware that the administrator may have little influence when "*they* put their foot down" - which is often.

Change the scenario. Have the board (owner or executive director) consist of individuals who ARE MANAGED. This board sees their role as a passive one, or it is hamstrung by the number of members or the infrequency of its meetings. In one facility, there were 22 members on the board who only met once every three months due to the distance each member had to travel. With that number and the few meetings, the agenda was long and a number of issues were out-dated by the time the board dealt with them. You can imagine the effectiveness of a group that size.

A board where its members ARE MANAGED is not comfortable in dealing with any conflict situations within the facility or taking any risks. The administrator takes the problem and solutions presented by the department heads to the board. The board's response is always - "OK" (heads bobbing in unison). Of course the minutes of the meetings are sketchy and non-descript. Three months later the administrator experiences some problems with the program implemented and returns to the board for support. Their response "What program are you talking about?" The administrator proceeds to review what was discussed in the past meeting. The minutes are too vague to recall what was previously said. The administrator receives little if any support to defend the program.

The administrator becomes "gun shy." When he began, he was assertive and creative. Now staff see his actions and decisions as more guarded. The reason for the shift is simple. Without the necessary backing, he is hesitant to stand "out on the limb" by himself.

The idiosyncrasies of the board can become even more complicated when a few of its members MUST MANAGE and the rest ARE MANAGED. One or two individuals then dominate the board. The administrator frequently finds certain members of the board informally support him when discussing an issue together, but in the board meeting they never say a word. He finds he frequently answers to only one or two board members who have the rest under their control.

THE DIRECTOR OF RESIDENT CARE

The impact of ineffective management styles can be anywhere and everywhere in the organization. You can have a board where its members are EFFECTIVE MANAGERS, along with an administrator and most department heads who are EFFECTIVE MANAGERS, but the director of resident care is the exception. If she has a style where she MUST MANAGE, most of the organization will run smoothly except for the nursing department.

At a department head meeting all department heads are given instructions on implementing a new program. Over the next few weeks, the majority of department heads implement the program by assisting their staff not only to understand its importance and what is expected, but also determining when, how and who will do it.

The director of resident care approaches her staff differently. She tells her staff "We have been told to implement a new program. I want it done as quickly as possible, there should be no problems. It is a simple request." This director of resident care has little sensitivity to the problems and needs of her staff. She does not communicate the rationale for the program, believing it is obvious to all why it needs to be done. Her expectation is that her request to do it should be incentive enough. Staffs' lack of freedom to express their problems results in their running ragged to fulfill her instructions. It is not surprising the nursing department demonstrates some difficulties with the new program while other departments have it running smoothly.

The dynamics change again if the director of resident care IS MANAGED. After being told about the new program at the department head meeting, she returns to her unit managers and says "The administrator said (it is always 'the administrator said') that we have to implement this new program in our department. I don't know if it will work but we are going to give it a real try aren't we?"

This director of resident care does not want any conflict. She approaches every situation in a cautious, "wishy-washy" manner. She then returns to the department head meeting reporting problems other department heads have not experienced. Her excuses always sound legitimate "We have worked hard in nursing to try and implement what was asked. Unfortunately, the unit managers are saying that evening and night shifts are too busy. I've tried to tell them that is not an excuse, but you know how they are? I'll keep working on it." She is always delegating blame, and never willing to take a stand on any issues or responsibility for any problems.

THE UNIT MANAGER

An organization can have the board, the administrator and all department heads as EFFECTIVE MANAGERS, but a unit manager may be the exception. A unit manager who IS MANAGED does not deal well with conflict.

Imagine that the unit manager on the evening shift is a manager who IS MANAGED. A staff member working on that shift is doing something wrong. Would that unit manager correct him? Not likely. Being uncomfortable with conflict will only encourage her to avoid the issue. When the staff member is working at one end of the unit, she will remain at the other. She believes that if she doesn't see it, she doesn't have to deal with it. Even if by chance she does stumble onto a staff member doing something wrong, she will always pretend she didn't see it. If uncovered, her excuses for not correcting staff are many "I am responsible for taking care of medication and charting, not to supervise staff" or "There isn't enough time in the day to do everything. I am too busy to watch the staff all the time." In either case it is delegating blame - a belief that it is the director of resident care's job to discipline staff or it is not her fault that they keep her so busy.

Back to our original example. A new program is to be implemented in the nursing department. The director of resident care is an EFFECTIVE MANAGER and ensures that her unit managers understand the program and together they determine the steps necessary to implement it successfully. The afternoon unit manager who IS MANAGED has a different outcome. As soon as one or more staff complain that they can't do it for whatever reason, she backs away. When questioned by her manager why afternoons are not following through with the program like the other shifts, her response is "We are just too busy on afternoons to do what you are asking. I can't be everywhere all the time to watch the staff to make sure they are doing this on top of all of my medications and charting. You don't know what it is like." The merry-go-round goes round and round.

On the flip side, we have an afternoon unit manager who MUST MANAGE. She believes nursing staff cannot be trusted to do their jobs unless they are constantly "supervised." She gives none of her staff any freedoms to waiver from the structure she has implemented and doesn't invite their input on any decision making on how the unit is run. When she is asked to implement the program, she ignores the directions set by the director of resident care and the other unit managers and instead just "lays down the law." In fact her staff are not even told of the "why" for the program, only how they are going to do it.

Management problems can come from anywhere in the organization. No matter what your management style, it will be effected by the manager above, the manager below and the manager next to you.

SUMMARY

Being an EFFECTIVE MANAGER is not something that occurs because a person has a title. Before leaving this section, it is important to look at yourself. There is no use reading any more of this book if you do not take the time to answer a few basic questions.

What type of a manager are you?

What do you do that limits your effectiveness as a manager?

How have you as a manager contributed to the problems experienced in your organization?

How do you view your staff and their importance?

How do you see your role in ensuring the organization is run effectively?

Without answering these questions, you might as well put the book down. The solution to effective management is the ability to first challenge one's own attitudes and determine one's own areas for growth before turning to our staff. The complexities and pressures of our setting are great enough without denying that we may be part of the problem.

Chapter Four

STAFFING DYNAMICS

The same limitations and cautions apply when we discuss staff as they did for managers. The following is a general portrayal of three levels of staff performance. It is not to suggest that all staff are exactly as described or that staff fit into only one group. Staff are as complex as managers. The goal is to crystallize what can be encountered in order to demonstrate the effects of peer pressure and staffing dynamics.

To discuss staffing dynamics requires differentiating staff into three groups - positive, average and negative. These groups are not that clearly separated. It is more of a continuum, where some average lean towards the positive and some lean towards the negative.

POSITIVE---------------AVERAGE---------------NEGATIVE

Positive staff can be powerful individuals in any organization if they are supported properly. They will give a 100% of themselves in their work. Their primary work goal is quality of life for their residents. When these staff are on duty, there is little concern about what is happening on the unit. Usually what they are responsible for runs smoothly.

Average staff; are those who will perform a good days work under the right circumstances. They are followers rather than leaders, shying away from conflict whenever possible. They are more comfortable having their day outlined for them rather than having to make decisions about their role.

Then there are the *negative* staff. The characteristics of the negative staff can vary from those who are STRUCTURED, to those who become DEAD WOOD, to RESCUERS and SABOTEURS.

CHARACTERISTICS OF THE NEGATIVE STAFF

1) Those who are STRUCTURED

This is the person who works in our setting for one reason only - money. Don't get me wrong, all of us work to get paid. No one would invest forty hours per week, fifty weeks of the year in any job without such a reward. However, many of our staff take their responsibilities beyond monetary gains. They see what they do more as a profession, not just a job. Their goal is the well-being of the residents and they are willing to adapt what they do to enhance that person's quality of life.

Staff who are STRUCTURED see their job only as a "job." Their primary goal is to get the job done - putting in their eight hours doing only what they have to do. They invest as little energy, time and emotion as possible. Their perception is not resident oriented, but task oriented. Attempting to make what they do mechanical, where today is the same as yesterday and tomorrow the same as today.

This staff member mechanizes his job by instilling structure, rules and routines that he will not easily alter for any reason. He approaches the bath schedule by virtually lining the residents up and saying "Your bath is at 0700, yours at 0710, yours at 0720, . . ." This type of staff member will not change his routine merely on the request of a resident or peer, but only on the demand of his immediate manager. Even then he will try to lapse to his old routine if not closely monitored. Without being controlled, the STRUCTURED staff will attempt to control any unit.

Any new manager who believes that she is the "boss" will soon learn that the role is constantly challenged. On the units, there often exists a number of "unwritten rules." The one that fascinates me the most is - "All beds are to be done by 1100 hours." When staff are asked why all beds have to be done by 1100 hours, they will often respond - "It is policy." My next question seems logical - "What policy? Where is it written?" Their response "Oh it is not written. We have just been doing it like that for years." I had to keep this going "Who said you should be doing it like that?" "THEY!" If you could only find out who "they" are.

Unwritten rules - beds to be made by 1100, baths by 1000, coffee break by 1030 - are created and religiously maintained by those staff who are STRUCTURED. They know exactly what they are doing

69

tomorrow morning at 0915 hours. That is not an indication of their organizational skills. All of us plan our day, but the majority of us are flexible enough to adjust those plans if something more important arises. The STRUCTURED staff attempt to follow their routine regardless of the demands of the moment. They show little or no flexibility.

The effects of their approach and attitude can best be demonstrated when the STRUCTURED staff are assigned to a mentally impaired resident.

If at the start of a shift, you know who was on duty the previous shift by the amount of wandering and agitated behavior of your mentally impaired residents, then you know what I am talking about.

The mentally impaired are our barometers to the quality of care being provided. They do not respond well to an imposed structure. Pressuring the mentally impaired to perform only intensifies their anxiety, resulting in an increase in aggressive outbursts and wandering behavior. Their inability to identify day, time, faces, events, etc. makes it impossible for them to remember or even respond to any set routine, other than their own at the moment. The effectiveness of staff working with this clientele is dictated by that person's ability to be flexible - the ability to adjust the care routine based on the individual resident's needs and abilities. STRUCTURED staff do not practice such flexibility. Their approach is to ignore the abilities or desires of any resident for the sake of completing the job.

However, you will find that the STRUCTURED staff would rather work with the mentally impaired rather than the cognitively well when such flexibility is not required nor enforced. The reasoning for their attraction to the mentally impaired may be explained by the following:

Imagine that you are a mentally impaired resident.

I brought in your breakfast tray and placed it out of your sight for 20 minutes, would you question me about it?

You are a cognitively well resident.

I brought your breakfast tray to you and your coffee was cold, would you challenge me on it?

You are a mentally impaired resident.

Your bath is normally scheduled for 1000 hours. I take you for your bath at 0830 hours, would you know the difference?

You are a cognitively well resident.

Your bath is normally scheduled for 1000 hours, and I try to take you for your bath at 0930 hours, would you question me about it?

STRUCTURED staff can easily manipulate the majority of the mentally impaired residents. Many of these residents will not know the difference from one staff member to another, from one shift to another. The cognitively well residents on the other hand will compare the care and the freedoms they were provided during this shift to the last person on duty, not easily accepting any restrictions.

This diversity in care can be demonstrated in another way. You will find on some units the cognitively well residents will watch the entrance of the unit at the change of each shift, to see who is coming on duty, so they will know what they can have or be allowed to do for that shift. They know if a STRUCTURED staff member is on duty, there will be little flexibility over the next eight hours, and only a basic routine of eating, washing, changing and going to bed will result.

What causes a staff member to become STRUCTURED is very unique to our setting. Many direct line staff in long term care have had little or no formal training. Usually their indoctrination to the job and its demands occur only after they are hired. In the beginning, this person may have started the job with considerable enthusiasm, only to have that desire and outlook quickly shattered as reality sets in.

Relate it to your own experience. In nurse's training, how many students were there at the start of the program compared to how many who graduated? When I taught in the nursing diploma program, approximately one hundred students would start first year but only about sixty would graduate. Why such a dramatic loss in enrollment? There are a number of reasons:

⇒ *Some of the students became disheartened.* They had a very glamorous and even grandiose belief of the role of a nurse. That misconception was quickly dispelled when they were required to carry their first bed pan. So they quit of their own accord.

⇒ *Others just couldn't "cut it."* Either they were unable to perform the physical care required or scholastically they could not meet the requirements, so they were asked to leave the program or they failed.

A common rationale for many who seek employment in long term care is that they like "old people." Some have the delusion that working in our setting involves helping "nice old people." They expect all of our residents to be similar to those people of the same age who they knew in the community, who were appreciative of any help received and easy to relate to. What they encounter can be quite a shock.

They are now required to care for "old people" experiencing complicated problems. They are expected to meet a wide range of needs (psychological, emotional, physical, social, spiritual, etc.) and deal with a variety of complex problems (physical and verbal aggression, death, disfigurement, an array of psychological problems, confusion and disorientation, inappropriate sexual behavior and so on). It is more than some bargained for. They find the demands placed on them go beyond their comprehension or ability. So what do they do? Leave!

In our setting, a direct line staff member who is untrained or has minimal training makes substantially more than untrained workers in other service oriented occupations. In addition, the job includes significant benefits and securities that could not be found in many other places with minimal standards for employment. What else could this person do that would provide the same monetary rewards? Work in a retail store at half the wage and with little security?

The STRUCTURED staff member is a person who finds himself stuck. He does not want to walk away from what he is making, but doesn't particularly like what he is doing, or even worse, is emotionally or mentally unable to handle the pressures of the job. So he creates a defense that makes the job tolerable. He dilutes his role to a simple mechanical process. Completing his job in an assembly line fashion, he is then only required to invest a minimal amount of energy, thought and emotion. The routine becomes a barrier or buffer that allows him to view the resident as nothing more than an object, a means to an end, and that end being a job that requires him to perform only basic physical care.

Why this person is tolerated and allowed to remain in the facility is simple - he "does his work." He performs the basic requirements of physical care adequately - bathing, feeding, dressing, etc. - but he will go no further. He cannot comprehend, or refuses to become involved with the *other* aspects of care - emotional support, allowing the resident to be part of the decision making, quality of life issues, etc. These are the abstract components of care that are difficult to define, difficult to measure and difficult to hold staff accountable for.

2) The SABOTEUR

This staff member often develops in a facility where there is inconsistent management. Imagine that the unit manager on the afternoon shift is one who IS MANAGED. I am a staff member working who is doing something wrong. We know that a manager who IS MANAGED does not deal with conflict well. It is not surprising that she does not correct me on my performance. In fact she has avoided dealing with that issue for some time.

You are now assigned as the unit manager to replace her. You are an EFFECTIVE MANAGER who has no difficulty confronting staff on poor performance. On your first shift you see me doing that thing that is wrong. You immediately correct me. My response is "I've always done it like that. The previous unit manager didn't say anything about it. Everybody else does it that way." Based on the inconsistencies experienced, I feel justified in believing that your actions are personal - why else would you correct me, when nobody else has. This can be complicated even further.

You have been a manager in the facility for two years. There are considerable differences in management styles and no accountability of any managers in how they perform their jobs. This results in each shift being run differently. What occurs when staff rotate from manager to manager is that they receive conflicting instructions and expectations. When staff return to your shift, you find it necessary to constantly confront them on what you expect and how they are to perform. In fact over the past two years you have repeatedly corrected staff on the very same issue you are now correcting me. This is the hundredth time in two years that you have had to tell someone about that one issue. How objective are you? Your frustration causes you to become somewhat emotional when you confront me. I can easily interpret your actions as personal - "She doesn't talk to anyone else like that." The perception of your actions being personal initiates a counter response - "I'll get even." This becomes the SABOTEUR - a person who believes he has been unjustly "kicked" and his only recourse is to "kick back."

The need for revenge creates some bizarre behaviors. In one setting a staff member believed he was unjustly reprimanded and the reason for the reprimand was his manager "had something against" him. The day after the reprimand, this staff member went into the staff washroom, stuffed a roll of toilet paper down the toilet, flushed it and walked out. When asked why he acted that way, he responded "they deserved it for what they did to me." His belief was - they "kicked me," I'll just "kick them back."

The SABOTEUR becomes an effective passive/aggressor. He makes the decision that no matter what is asked of him, he will not cooperate. What protects him in his job is that he does not outwardly demonstrate to managers how he actually feels. He performs his duties adequately and usually doesn't show any blatant resistance.

Some saboteurs become effective performers, being very devious and slippery. They play a game where they ensure their performance is acceptable when any manager is in sight, but when out of sight their conduct is deplorable, taking every opportunity to "stir things up," going out of their way to make sure things don't work.

Some managers may be deceived. At a meeting, the SABOTEUR may appear positive and creative in suggesting solutions to a specific problem, or when a manager is around they are seen being very compassionate to the residents. Staff see something entirely different. They experience a person who is constantly "bad mouthing" everything and everyone in the organization and who is very insensitive towards the residents.

The SABOTEUR is always wary of a manager's presence. Their goal is not to get caught again, but they are always trying to get even. When other members of the team complain about this person's attitudes or work habits, they may get little support from managers who don't see that same person in that way.

In an organization where management is inconsistent, the unit manager may find little support from upper management when requesting disciplinary actions towards a SABOTEUR. Top management may not agree with what the unit manager sees. In such a setting, when the top manager is required to question other unit managers who ARE MANAGED about this person's behavior and attitude, these managers may simply respond "He's OK," attempting to avoid potential conflict. The effective manager may be stuck with a good actor, but a poor employee. In any event, with the SABOTEUR, watch your back.

3) The RESCUER

The RESCUER is a "sweet" person - bitter sweet. This individual cannot be considered a caregiver as we know the term, but instead a RESCUER. This is a person who gets a personal high by making people dependent on them.

Imagine that we have a resident who has not fed herself for a year. Through the team's assessment, it is decided that she can probably feed herself with a spoon. The RESCUER will sit in the team conference and appear to support the direction set by the team. However, when the RESCUER goes into that resident's room, the RESCUER does what she thinks is right, regardless of what the team has decided. This person has a very syrupy response to all residents. The RESCUER speaks and approaches residents in a condescending manner, always stroking them and calling them "deary," "sweetheart," "honey bun." Her response to the resident who is to be encouraged to feed herself with a spoon is "Mrs. Jones, they say you should feed yourself. You shouldn't have to feed yourself at your age dear, that's why I'm here. I'll feed you, but don't tell anyone." After feeding the resident, the RESCUER walks out of that room, head held high and chest out, a look that almost says "Well, I helped another one!"

The motivation for this staff member is not based on what will benefit the resident, but what will satisfy her need for self gratification. Why I call this person a RESCUER is simple. She is the type of person that when she sees you swimming in the lake, she will swim out to save you from drowning whether you are drowning or not, just for the feeling that she has helped.

As a manager you will have a difficult time making this person accountable for her actions. When you confront her about feeding Mrs. Jones, her response will be "I was only trying to help." If you are not careful in what you do, it will become a losing situation. Let it go by and you have sanctioned her actions, giving her permission to do what she wants regardless of what the team decides (the actions of the manager who IS MANAGED). Confront her (the manager who MUST MANAGE) and you will find she will interpret your actions to the rest of the staff as unjustified "She reprimanded me for helping Mrs. Jones."

The RESCUER will often remain in some facilities because her intentions are misinterpreted by others. Those who see her periodically (family, upper management, residents, etc.) may believe she is "good with the residents." They interpret her actions as a demonstration of her concern and her fussing over the residents as a reflection of her caring. They are unaware that what she accomplishes is to smother the residents, stripping them of their independence and individuality.

4) Those who are DEAD WOOD

The creation of this person is probably the most disheartening. You have heard the term "staff burnout." In our business, burnout is not an abstract disease, it is a potential reality. There are two kinds of burnout - acute and chronic. We all suffer from periodic acute burnout. There are those days when you have to be at work for 0700 hours, you wake at 0655 hours, turn to the clock, then look up and say, "Lord, could you have a little earthquake today. Just something to gobble up the facility! You can spit it back up tomorrow." Those are the days where it is hard to get started. After a half hour at work you find yourself going at full speed.

Chronic burnout is when a person wakes each morning for work and says to himself "I hate this job." Yet he still keeps dragging himself to work. When asked why he stays at a job he doesn't like, he will tell you "I'm stuck." Those who become DEAD WOOD develop the same rationale as those who are STRUCTURED. Sticking to a job he doesn't like because of job security, money, pension plan, sick time, preferred shift, etc. His response is always the same "How can I walk away from all of that?" So he doesn't.

The difference from those who are STRUCTURED to those who become DEAD WOOD is obvious. DEAD WOOD were probably very competent caregivers at one time. This staff member just stayed too long in a job that he found repetitive. He has become bored and his boredom has diluted his drive and enthusiasm. Or worse, the facility in which he works has not supported him in what he does. He has become tired of fighting the system, so he has given up and only "puts in time."

Staff who are DEAD WOOD find that every eight hour shift seems endless. When at work, he constantly wishes he were somewhere else. Any resident who puts additional demands on him only increases his frustration. In fact the care team as well usually loses its tolerance with this type of staff member. They find that he frequently does not complete his work and is always asking for help from everyone else. Many learn that unless someone is checking on him constantly, little or nothing is done. Staff who are DEAD WOOD have no enthusiasm, no caring, no resistance - nothing.

The tolerance by peers and managers of this individual is generated from his previous work history - in "his day" he was good. Now that he has changed, many are reluctant to confront him, thinking that he may snap back and resume the performance pattern they once admired in him. Unfortunately it may not occur. This staff member is in a downward spiral, his apathy only initiates further apathy in others.

PROFILE OF THE NEGATIVE STAFF

I know what you were doing as you read the descriptions of the negative staff. You placed the names and faces of some of your staff to them. No organization is without negative staff. Negative staff are like crab grass in your lawn. You can work all you want one year to get rid of them, only to find the next spring they are back again. The only thing that varies from facility to facility is the configuration of staff mix.

Some facilities have 10% positive, 80% average and 10% negative, where other facilities have 10% positive, 60% average and 30% negative.

The negative staff in a supportive, well functioning organization have very little power. In such a setting, the staff supports are clearly defined and well implemented. Staff know where they stand regarding decision making and accountability, and communication and recognition is clear, regular and direct. When staff are excited about what they do and where they do it, the negative staff have little edge. On the other hand, organizations weak in such supports may find themselves constantly influenced by the actions and attitudes of the negative staff.

By the way, negative staff rarely see themselves as negative. In fact they will usually profess that they are doing the best job they can, given what they have to work with. They will place fault for any limitations they have in providing care or doing their job on the organization and its managers (remember the rational for the psychological game of "bitching" described earlier). They always paint a bleak picture about their work place to anyone who will listen. The comments are common:

> *"This place doesn't care about its staff."*
> *"No one listens to what we have to say."*
> *"No one recognizes our accomplishments."*

There seems no end to the litany they profess. Their description is not intended as <u>constructive criticism</u> - a mechanism intended to provide an opportunity to seek solutions to existing problems. Instead it is <u>destructive</u> - exaggerating the flaws of the organization and denying its strengths. Negative staff will always tell you what will not work and rarely discuss what might.

The negative staff create for themselves a self-fulfilling prophecy. They frequently receive little recognition because they often do very little to merit it. Few managers and staff in the organization are comfortable with them because of their attitude and behavior. In fact, many may cringe when a negative staff member walks onto the unit or into a meeting. Many find the negative staff very difficult to talk to and their constant complaining about everything is something others may not agree with or may not want to always hear.

It is difficult for anyone to admit that one's own actions may be the cause of what one is experiencing. It is like the alcoholic who does not believe he is an alcoholic. As long as he maintains that belief, it would be difficult to convince him to change his behavior and stop drinking. Such an admission requires considerable insight into one's problems. When that occurs, there is then the need to find a way to change what is happening. A negative staff member who does not see himself as negative will not admit that he needs to change his behavior and attitude. Instead he will believe that the reason things are as bad as they are is because of everyone else. Once that person can justify that his behavior is reactive to an external force beyond his control, he then stops looking for solutions. He sees the facility as negative and therefore rationalizes why he acts the way he does - negatively.

The belief that this is a terrible place to work may be accurate. Unfortunately, such places do exist. There are still some managers who treat their staff poorly. However the perceptions of the negative staff in many instances are exaggerated. When asked to evaluate the facility, negative staff will only sight the weaknesses - there's too much work, there's not enough equipment, no one tells you that you do a good job, there's too much pressure, etc. They will rarely define any strengths let alone possible solutions. Yet talking to the positive or the average staff in the same facility you will usually find that they do not see it in the same way. They will identify the organization's weaknesses, tell you about its strengths, and usually provide their suggestions on how the organization and care may be improved.

What is important for the negative staff is to justify their belief system. Their interpretation of their surroundings is their rationale for their actions. To have that belief system proven wrong is to force change, or to at least take ownership that what they are doing is the result of their own decisions and not totally the fault of others.

Imagine that you are a positive staff member and have established a close relationship with three residents under your care. Throughout the year you have taken each of them shopping or out to supper on your own time. You frequently bring in things that you know they like, paying for them from your own pocket. Such actions on the part of any staff are commendable. Staff who add a little more to enhance a resident's quality of life should be encouraged to maintain that effort. For many of our residents, staff may become the main player as their "significant other."

When a positive staff member excels in such a manner it is a direct threat to the negative staff:

How can one staff member give so much and another so little in the same location?

If I am a negative staff member, your actions concern me. When others see what you are doing, they may want me to do the same. Negative staff do not want to do anything "extra." However, most negative staff are not that blatant in expressing their personal reasons for wanting to stop other staff from doing more than what is required. Such an action would be too obvious to others and provide an opportunity to hold them accountable. Instead they are much more subtle. They camouflage their motives by expressing their concerns in a way that appears as though they are taking care of others.

As a negative staff member, I would never say to you "Don't do that because I don't want to have to do it." or "You make me look bad when you do extra things and I don't." What would probably be expressed is "Why are *you* doing that? Nobody gives a damn. *You* won't get anything for it. No one cares." How do you argue with someone who appears to be looking out for your best interests?

You can hear it almost anywhere at any time. If the afternoon shift is asked to do something extra without having any additional staff, the negative staff would never say "I've had enough of that." They wouldn't take such ownership in their statement. Instead their response would probably be "OK people, *we've* had enough. *We're* not going to take it any more. *We'll* only do what we have to." That pseudo caring of others makes it difficult for many to challenge the negative staff.

Once this person has convinced himself that his perception is right, he has also justified his behavior and the power struggle begins. The negative against the positive, each with opposing views, each believing their perception is accurate. The workplace now has the makings of a very unique and complex psychological process of group manipulation. As we will discover, the power over who will win the battle is in the hands of the organization and its management staff.

THE STRUGGLE FOR POWER

The negative staff are in a constant power struggle with the positive staff. To clarify this, imagine the following:

The two of us are direct line caregivers. You are a positive staff member and I am a negative one. You walk by the room of a mentally impaired resident at the same time as I am trying to stand her up from her chair to take her to the bathroom. My approach is obviously sharp and abrupt and the resident is resisting me.

You enter the room and ask me what I'm doing (this takes a very confident and assertive staff member to take such action). I respond "What do you mean. I'm taking her to the bathroom like I always do." It is obvious to you that my approach is causing the resident to resist. To rectify that you offer to help "I have found if you approach this resident in a certain manner, she will not fight you. Let me show you." You kneel down in front of the resident so she can see you. You gently touch her arm, talk to her for a few moments to calm her down. You ask if she would like to go to the bathroom and ask again to ensure she understands. Then you gradually draw her up from the chair and take her to the bathroom without her fighting.

Staff confronting staff on such matters is not a common occurrence, let alone confronting a negative staff member. The incident is not closed yet.

Both of us know that it is a waste of effort to challenge each other directly. We know that we are drastically different from each other in our perceptions of the job and how it is to be done and too committed in our beliefs to change our minds. Unfortunately, when and if you do challenge me, I cannot let it go by. To correct my approach with this mentally impaired resident makes me look "bad." It implies that my actions caused her agitation rather than my belief that she is always like this because she is confused. What you are in fact telling me is to change how I do things. That leaves me no choice but to repudiate your actions - *I need to get back at you.*

Where I will get you is at coffee break. At break, I will pull up a chair to a group of staff and say "Do you know what she did? Who does she think she is talking to me like that." I will "rip a strip of hide" off you and you won't even know it. The weapon of the negative staff in this battle for control is "bitching." You have now become my target.

Now "bitching" can be a worthwhile process in a problem solving situation. If a group of people have a great deal of pent up emotions over a problem or situation, their objectivity may be restricted. "Bitching" can be a way of releasing those underlying emotions to allow clear-headed analysis to solve those problems. The negative staff on the other hand are not seeking solutions to the problems they express. Their "bitching" is a means of justifying their behavior and attitude.

When I say "This place doesn't give a damn about you. They don't care. They don't listen. . ." I am not looking for a way to solve those concerns. Instead, I want others to see a picture of where they work that advocates doing the least, staying detached, being structured, being suspicious. Once I have established that perception, I have given myself permission to do the things I do. When a group sits and listens to my "bitching," without challenging what I am saying, their silence can be interpreted on my part as agreement. It is even more effective when two negative staff are involved in the "bitching." Each feeds off the other to paint the darkest picture possible.

When I describe your actions to others, I do not suggest that I had any problem with the resident that required your help. I indicate nothing that may suggest that I need to change my approach. Instead I postulate that your motives were personal - "She's always showing off. She thinks she's better than any of us." What I propose is that you would do this to anyone, not to help the resident but to show that you believe you are more skilled than anyone else. To others it sounds as though I am taking care of them by warning them to watch out for you.

The rationale for the "bitcher" to discredit you in front of others is to make you "look bad." That dilutes your power and influence over others in two ways. First, once you encounter the repercussions of my "bitching," you will probably be less willing to challenge me in the future. In that way I will eventually be allowed to do what I want without someone like you pressuring me to change. Without my making it uncomfortable for you to confront me, you may become a constant "thorn in my side." Consistently conflicting with me in how I describe this place, how I approach the residents, how I perform care, etc. Each time I say or do something negative, you would counter with something

82

positive. By making you the target of my "bitching," my intention is to "shut you down."

The second thing I attempt to accomplish by "bitching" is to lessen your credibility with others. When I describe you as one of "them," a person who can't be trusted, who is always "sucking up to management," etc., those who listen may believe me or at least become suspicious enough of your motives and may hesitate in following you. I force positive staff to continually defend their actions to other staff based on "hearsay." The more staff I can get to listen to me, the less they may listen to you.

THE EFFECTS ON THE POSITIVE STAFF

The positive staff are not only assaulted directly by the negative staff, but they are also affected indirectly by what they see happening to the residents. The positive staff usually have excellent insight and ability to encourage residents to become independent. Unfortunately, what they experience is constant interference from the negative staff in achieving that goal.

Take the resident discussed earlier who has not fed herself for a year. After a thorough assessment of this person's abilities, it is determined that she could probably feed herself with a spoon if given the needed direction and support. Once initiated, it takes you and the other staff on duty the first three days to motivate her to pick the spoon up, the next two days for her to start feeding herself. You are off duty for two days and when you return you find that some staff continued to feed her, disregarding the program that you and the others initiated. Who fed her? Obviously, the negative staff.

The SABOTEUR would feed her to take revenge by ensuring the program didn't work. The RESCUER would feed her because she couldn't stand to see anyone struggle. The person who is STRUCTURED feeds her because she has always done it that way. The person who is DEAD WOOD feeds her because it takes less time and energy - "Do you know what it means to get her to feed herself? You have to bring in the soup, then the main course, then the desert, etc. She has it all over her, the table, the floor. Heck you can feed her in four minutes and thirteen seconds flat."

When there is little accountability, there can be little consistency. The lack of accountability allows any staff member to do what he wants, when he wants, regardless of the direction set by the team or the desires of the resident. For the positive staff it is four steps forward and three steps back. In fact in some instances it may be four steps forward and five back. It is difficult to convince this resident to feed herself, when she knows others will feed her when you are not around.

One wonders how long the care team can maintain their momentum, continually encouraging this resident to feed herself, only to find their initiatives negated by others who feed her. Eventually the majority of staff will probably decide it is a waste of time and feed her regardless of what is indicated on the care plan.

As a positive staff member you know that the team has abandoned the program not on the basis of this resident's abilities, but due to the lack of consistency. You know this lady's potential cannot be achieved regardless of what you do personally to support or encourage her. How would that awareness affect you? It is not surprising that many of the positive staff in such a setting soon become frustrated. The realistic goals set for the residents are not met because of the influences of only a few staff.

TIPPING THE SCALES

The positive staff are constantly being challenged. The deciding factor identifying who will win this struggle for power is primarily in the hands of the organization and its management staff. Return to our initial scenario in this section. A staff member establishes a close relationship with three residents, doing extra things for them on her own time. As a negative staff member I constantly harass that person, questioning her on her actions - "What are you doing that for? No one gives a damn. You won't get anything for it." What occurs when you never hear - "You are doing a good job." Recognition for one's accomplishments is essential for motivation. When lacking, it becomes difficult to maintain one's enthusiasm and excitement in any workplace.

The more instances there are to support the perceptions of the negative staff, the more power they have. If no one says to you "You are doing a good job," then the negative staff are proven right - "I told you no one cares." Once I have something to substantiate my claims, I can now become self-righteous "I have been telling everyone for years that *they* (management) don't give a damn about *us* (staff)," and you have nothing concrete to dispute my accusation.

Staff become confused. They are told that the organization's philosophy is quality of life, but when staff attempt to achieve that goal by surpassing the normal routine, all they get in return is the furor of the negative staff. In an organization where the negative staff are unchallenged, they can make the positive staff member's life in the facility very uncomfortable.

These dynamics create a downward spiral. The more the organization withholds support of the positive staff and does not hold the negative staff accountable, the more credibility the negative staff have with the average and even the positive staff. Many may begin thinking "She was right about the last thing she told us. She might be right about this one."

THE FORMATION OF CLIQUES

Eventually staff cliques will develop within the facility. The members and purpose of these cliques can best be seen in the staff lounge during breaks. The negative staff will sit with a specific group of staff at one table and the positive staff will be sitting with others at another table.

This intentional separation is due to the continual "bitching" of the negative staff. The positive staff become tired of the "bitching." They don't agree with what is being said, and are weary of challenging the negative staff on nearly every issue. Furthermore, most positive staff believe that a break is for a break, not to talk about work. The negative staff maintain the same avoidance tactics. They would rather sit with other negative staff or average staff who will listen.

Cliques can be found on the unit as well. The negative and positive staff will try to avoid each other as much as possible. When they are working on the same unit during the same shift, they will attempt to separate themselves through the resident assignments.

Imagine a unit with four direct line staff. One of those four is obviously positive and another very negative. If free to assign work duties, the positive staff member will team up with the peer she can best relate to and the negative staff member will team up with the one she can best relate to. If such a separation occurs, you will see the difference in performance as soon as you enter the unit. Excellent care on one half of the unit, mediocre to poor care on the other.

IDENTIFYING THE CAUSALITIES

As these dynamics intensify, certain characteristics become evident:

- it becomes harder and harder to develop a team atmosphere
- cliques occur among staff, some refusing to work with others
- programs are falling apart due to a lack of consistency
- realistic goals are not met
- personality conflicts overrule professional conduct
- the negative staff attempt to take more and more liberties

Without intervention, many of the positive staff will eventually become disheartened and give up fighting.

If you have been in such a setting, and most of us have, you know very well what it is like. You have the feeling that most of your energies are invested in fighting the system. It is like hitting your head against a brick wall. After a while your head begins to hurt. The stress encountered takes a physical, mental and emotional toll.

Physically, positive staff start utilizing sick time. In fact sick time is an effective way to measure staff morale. As staff morale decreases, sick time increases. Sick time can become for some an avoidance response to stress. Individuals who have never taken sick time in the past, now use their accumulated sick time at an alarming rate. The rationale is simple. If one believes that it is no longer possible to change what is occurring, then the only option to deal with the increasing stress is to take a day away. The hope is that the extra day away from the work environment will help to regain their energy, motivation and drive. What they soon find is that one day away is not enough. They then take two, three and more for the slightest, if any, ailment.

As staff experience more stress, they even become emotionally drained. Every resident request is just another challenge that the positive staff feel they cannot meet. They find it increasingly harder and harder to give to the residents they care so much about.

Finally, the positive staff can change mentally. In time, it is quite possible that they too can become cynical. Staff who were the most excited, up-beat individuals start to sound and think like the negative staff. It is not uncommon for positive staff to spew out the sayings of the negative - "This is not going to work, why even bother" to any suggestion.

As the positive staff become exhausted fighting the system (or "beating their head against that brick wall,") some may simply "turn-off" in order to survive. They become DEAD WOOD. They virtually pull themselves out of the picture, making the decision to only coast - "I have had enough of this. I don't care about the team, programming, none of it any more. I will just put in my eight hours and that is all." They no longer take an active role within the team, in program development or anything else involving the unit due to the pressures they have encountered. Positive staff now become part of the problem.

There is another response. Some who are determined not to let go of their beliefs and principles of care make a healthier decision. They quit. They look for another place to work where they may be appreciated and supported in what they do. The facility sees an exodus of its best staff.

When the positive staff remove themselves from their active participation in either way, there is nobody left to conflict with the negative staff. The negative staff are now a major force for the manager to deal with in the organization.

SETTING LIMITS

The first response by many managers when discussing these staff dynamics may be "I have never seen it that bad." What has been described is the full scope of the process. The dynamics exist in a variety of dimensions and degree of intensity throughout the industry. No matter which level it is, it can become a very serious and deadly issue that is not easily rectified by any manager, regardless of his skills.

In one facility where the entire process described was at its peak, the care was deplorable, the staff morale pathetic. There existed an organizational tension that could be felt by everyone. Staff and managers talked in "us-them" terms. The staff sick time budget and injury compensation claims were uncontrollable. Staff turn-over was abnormally high. Resident abuse cases and injuries were frequent and often hidden and overlooked. Finally, the facility became so enveloped in scandal that the community demanded action. The decision was to discharge all existing managers and start anew.

The new administrator said to me "I don't understand it. I am a good manager. I listen and encourage others to share their ideas. I feel I am conscious of motivating and rewarding staff and have no problem setting a pace that staff can handle. Yet I have received more grievances in the time that I have been here than this facility has seen in the past 10 years. Why?" The answer is simple - the negative staff are not prepared to let go of their power. Once a manager begins telling staff they are important, encouraging them to express their concerns, assisting them in solving their problems, encouraging staff involvement in determining how to do their job - it evaporates the power the negative staff have worked so hard to attain.

It now becomes a <u>waiting game</u> - determining who can outlast who. Initially, this new manager needed to expect that everything he did would be discolored by the negative staff. He had to wait it out. It involved:

⇒ countering everything the negative staff did by establishing a positive and supportive environment to prove that trust was deserved (building that positive and strong staff/management relationship).

⇒ supporting the POSITIVE staff (to re-excite them).

⇒ ensuring that his managers were skilled and consistent (creating EFFECTIVE MANAGERS).

⇒ enforcing and communicating a strong and consistent message to empower staff (enhancing the confidence of the AVERAGE staff).

All of this was intended for one thing. To convince the majority of staff within his charge to trust again. To become open minded and receptive. To be ready for the necessary changes that would allow the organization to function effectively.

This manager did not allow events or the comments of others to dissolve his excitement. He turned this organization around. By his efforts and determination, his organization is now effective in its ability to provide quality of life for the residents who live there, and quality of work life for the staff and managers who worked there.

SUMMARY

The driving force that can affect organizational functioning is peer-on-peer pressure. What seems to be always present is a tug of war - the positive staff pulling to bring the care team to its maximum level of functioning (providing quality of life), and the negative staff pulling to bring the care team to a stand-still (custodial care). As we will see, some organizations and its management staff inadvertently throw their weight in favor of the negative staff. Without effective and consistent management skills and an organization that provides sufficient supports, the positive staff are pulled off balance, drawing the care team further from the goal of quality of life.

The suspense escalates
as the plot unfolds.

Chapter Five

ORGANIZATIONAL DYNAMICS AND THE MANAGER'S ROLE

We have identified three management styles:

1) The EFFECTIVE MANAGER has the ability and necessary skills to encourage staff motivation. Her style is one that assists others to function at their maximum potential by clearly defining goals and setting realistic expectations of performance. This person excites those who work with her.

2) The manager who IS MANAGED is governed by conflict and is uncomfortable with the demands of the job. This person attempts to avoid taking a stand, and delegates blame to others or external factors for any difficulties experienced. This person confuses those who work for him.

3) The manager who MUST MANAGE has a need to control both the situation and the people under his charge. This person does not trust others to perform their job without close supervision and is very opinionated in his decisions. If unchecked, his beliefs and actions will stifle the performance of staff. This person paralyzes those who work for him.

And also presented three groups of staff performance:

1) The Positive staff give 100% of themselves and are committed to what they do. They are resident oriented, attempting to enhance the quality of life for those under

their care. They are very skilled and insightful in performing their duties.

2) The Average staff complete a good day's work. They are not assertive, shying away from conflict and preferring that any decisions about their role be made by others.

3) The Negative staff include the STRUCTURED, SABOTEUR, RESCUER and DEAD WOOD. These are individuals whose motives are personal and whose performance is questionable. They are generally task oriented and if unchecked, their attitude and performance will cripple the care team and the organization .

We need to include a third group in our discussion of organizational dynamics in long term care. These are the cognitively well residents. In the text "Working with the Frail Elderly: Beyond the Physical Disability," I discussed three responses of the cognitively well residents: the Well Adjusted Response, the Withdrawn Response and the Aggressive Response. Here is a brief summary of those responses.

1) The Well Adjusted Response

This is a resident who responds positively to living in a long term care facility. He sees our place as "the next thing to heaven." His perception is based on a personal decision - regardless of what he has experienced, he has decided to make the best of what remains of his life - and he does.

2) The Aggressive Response

This resident has also made a decision about his life - "I have not changed, I am still the man I have been all my life and I will fight to prove to you and myself that I am still that man." This person tries to hold onto a lifestyle that no longer exists or a way of controlling that lifestyle that is no longer available. He denies any changes or losses he has experienced. He fights care, programming, life, change, anything and everything from the day he enters the building.

3) The Withdrawn Response

This is the resident who staff place in a chair when and where they want for as long as they want. They probably feed him, dress him and he shows little response. This resident has decided that what remains in his life is only time - he is simply waiting for death. This person believes that the losses and changes he has encountered at this point in his life have stripped him of any quality in life.

DEFINING THE DYNAMICS

An overview of the entire organization - staff, managers and residents would appear as follows:

> ### MANAGERS
> *IS MANAGED---EFFECTIVE MANAGERS---MUST MANAGE*
>
> ### STAFF
> *NEGATIVE-----AVERAGE-----POSITIVE*
>
> ### RESIDENTS
> *WITHDRAWN-----WELL ADJUSTED-----AGGRESSIVE*

THE IMPACT OF THE NEGATIVE STAFF

Considerable time has been spent discussing the effects of the negative staff on the organization. We can now identify their overall impact on the residents, on other staff, and on managers .

1) On Residents (Figure #12)

a) What effect does negative staff have on the Well Adjusted resident?

Frustrates them. The resident who has the ability and desire to decide his own lifestyle within the facility, experiences considerable frustration at having to constantly challenge the de-humanizing approach and attitude of the negative staff who impose their pre-determined rules and routines.

b) What effect does negative staff have on the Withdrawn resident?

Controls them. If negative staff tell the Withdrawn resident what to do, that person usually does it. This resident's apathetic state creates a compliance that allows the negative staff to freely manipulate him into any routine they desire.

c) What effect does negative staff have on the Aggressive resident?

Reinforces them. Both staff and the Aggressive resident are structured, neither willing to show any flexibility. The negative staff attempts to control a resident who himself wants control. For the Aggressive resident, it legitimizes his aggressive behavior. The unilateral and restrictive actions of the negative staff justifies his becoming angry in order to gain that control. Likewise the abrasive actions of the aggressive resident encourages negative staff to avoid involving the resident in any decision making. This resident is a direct challenge to the approach of this staff. In fact you may find some of the most intense, aggressive outbursts by this type of resident occurs when a negative staff member is on duty. It becomes a head-to-head confrontation - the resident demanding to do it his way and the staff member wanting it hers.

Impact of the Negative Staff on Residents

(Figure #12)

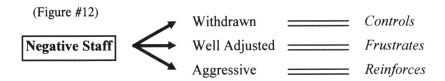

Negative Staff		Withdrawn	===	*Controls*
		Well Adjusted	===	*Frustrates*
		Aggressive	===	*Reinforces*

2) On Staff (Figure #13)

   a) What effect does negative staff have on negative staff?

      Reinforces them. The negative staff feed and reinforce other negative staff. They congregate into cliques where each supports the other in finding and magnifying the flaws within the organization.

   b) What effect does negative staff have on the average staff?

      Controls them. The average staff are uncomfortable with conflict and would rarely confront the negative staff. They will follow the direction of the strongest person on duty. If there are no controls placed on the negative staff within the organization, then this is the person they will follow.

   c) What effect does negative staff have on the positive staff?

      Frustrates them. No matter what the positive staff attempt to do, the negative staff will always try to undo it.

Impact of the Negative Staff on Staff

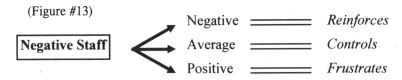

3) On Managers (Figure #14)

   a) What effect does the negative staff have on the manager who IS MANAGED?

      Controls them. The negative staff benefit from this manager's inability to deal with conflict. The manager who IS MANAGED will not assert himself in a conflict situation, and allows the negative staff free reign in what they do and how they do it.

b) What effect does the negative staff on the EFFECTIVE MANAGER?

Frustrates them. No matter what this manager attempts to initiate, the negative staff will try to undermine him.

c) What effect does the negative staff have on the manager who MUST MANAGE?

Reinforces them. When a positive staff member approaches a manager who MUST MANAGE with an idea, he shuts her down, making her feel uncomfortable, almost making her feel as if she must apologize for suggesting it. The negative staff use such incidents to reinforce their perception - "I told you nobody wants to listen to our ideas. We're just staff." The attitudes and actions of this manager provides the needed legitimacy to the negative staff member's "bitching." All staff on occasion have dealt with the manager who MUST MANAGE and have encountered just what the negative staff profess. That is why it is so hard for many to challenge how the negative staff describe the facility and how it is run. The negative staff take advantage of isolated instances created by this manager to make global statements about all managers and the organization in general.

Impact of the Negative Staff on Managers

(Figure #14)

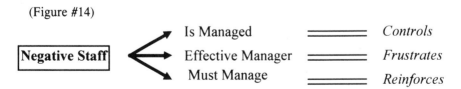

THE IMPACT OF THE MANAGER WHO MUST MANAGE

The impact of the manager who MUST MANAGE can be seen throughout the organization as well.

1) On Staff (Figure #15)
    a) What effect does the manager who MUST MANAGE have on positive staff?

> *Frustrates them.* Positive staff are creative people looking for ways to further enhance the quality of life for the residents. When positive staff approach the manager who MUST MANAGE and say "I have an idea," this manager responds "If I want your input I will ask you for it. Go back to the floor and do what you are supposed to be doing." This manager blocks the individual initiatives of positive staff, negating any contributions they may make.

    b) What effect does the manager who MUST MANAGE have on the average staff?

> *Controls them.* Average staff will not challenge a controlling manager. They yield to this manager's direction, regardless of the instructions given by another manager on a previous shift.

    c) What effect does the manager who MUST MANAGE have on the negative staff?

> *Reinforces them.* The attitudes and behaviors of the negative staff justify the beliefs and behavior of the manager who MUST MANAGE - take control or the job will not be done. To the other managers, the manager who MUST MANAGE repeatedly sights the negative staff as examples to prove that staff cannot be trusted to do their job without direct supervision. His broad brush analysis concludes that such

conduct can be expected of all staff advocating a need to treat all in the same manner.

Impact of the Manager Who Must Manage on Staff

(Figure #15)

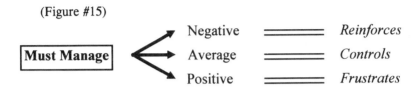

Must Manage	Negative	═══════	*Reinforces*
	Average	═══════	*Controls*
	Positive	═══════	*Frustrates*

2) On Managers (Figure #16)

   a) What effect does the manager who MUST MANAGE have on the manager who IS MANAGED?

> *Controls them.* The manager who IS MANAGED will not argue with this manager's analysis that staff cannot be trusted. His own attempt to camouflage his problems in dealing with conflict is to accept that staff are to blame just as the manager who MUST MANAGE professes.

   b) What effect does the manager who MUST MANAGE have on the EFFECTIVE MANAGER?

> *Frustrates them.* The EFFECTIVE MANAGER encourages a team approach that involves all levels of staff, only to find that the manager who MUST MANAGE counters it. The frustration for the EFFECTIVE MANAGER is created by the constant need to regain staff trust and re-motivate them to contribute.

   c) What effect does the manager who MUST MANAGE have on other managers who MUST MANAGE?

> *Reinforces them.* The manager who MUST MANAGE feeds the presumptions of other managers who MUST MANAGE.

Each finds support from the other in identifying and magnifying the flaws and limitations of staff.

Impact of the Manager Who Must Manage On Managers

(Figure #16)

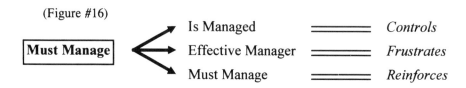

Must Manage

Is Managed ===== *Controls*

Effective Manager ===== *Frustrates*

Must Manage ===== *Reinforces*

3) On Residents (Figure #17)

Any actions by any manager will have direct impact on the care of the residents. The manager who IS MANAGED will not insist that a withdrawn resident become involved in any programming or insist that staff encourage her. The goal of this manager is to keep things quiet on the unit and the withdrawn resident accomplishes that well. Likewise, this manager cannot relate to an aggressive resident. She will avoid that resident and any staff problems surrounding his behavior as much as possible.

It is the manager who MUST MANAGE who has the most significant impact on residents.

a) What effect does the manager who MUST MANAGE have on the Withdrawn resident?

Controls them. The manager who MUST MANAGE dictates to staff what must be done, thereby determining what is best for the resident and disregarding the resident's previous lifestyle and present wishes. This manager justifies that what has to be done is done for the resident's own good. The condescending nature of this manager is to treat this resident more as a child than an adult.

b) What effect does the manager who MUST MANAGE have on the Well Adjusted resident?

Frustrates them. The manager who MUST MANAGE establishes a very structured environment. Staff are told on each shift what they are supposed to do and are not allowed to alter any of those instructions without this manager's permission. The Well Adjusted resident becomes frustrated with staff having to respond to every request with - "I don't know if I can do that, I'll have to ask the boss first."

c) What effect does the manager who MUST MANAGE have on the aggressive resident?

Reinforces them. Again both the manager who MUST MANAGE and the Aggressive resident want control. It becomes a head-to-head confrontation. This manager decides what is best for this resident and instructs the staff to do it regardless of the resident's response. The pressuring this resident encounters only intensifies his agitation. This resident outwardly shows his contempt by calling this manager a "Sergeant Major" and other terms that need not be expressed here.

Impact of the Manager Who Must Manage On Residents

(Figure #17)

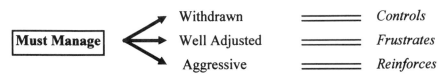

THE OVERALL IMPACT

Even though the number of negative staff and managers who MUST MANAGE may represent a small percentage within the facility, their influence can seriously contaminate any organization if it goes unchecked. Scan the following chart (Figure #18). You will find that the overall impact of the negative staff and the overall impact of the manager who MUST MANAGE on the organization is identical.

(Figure #18)

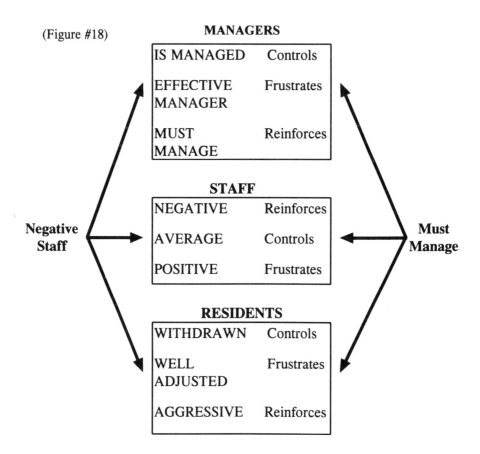

Many managers believe that the problems experienced within the organization can be blamed solely on the staff. That is not the case. The attitudes and behaviors of both the negative staff and the managers who MUST MANAGE have the exact same impact within the facility.

The key issue lies in the degree of effect. A negative staff member has little influence in the overall operation of the organization and level of care if the staff within that facility are supported. If poor performance is confronted and positive performance encouraged, then the power of the negative staff is minimal. On the other hand, the incompetent manager has devastating results regardless of the type of staff under his charge. If such a manager is unchecked, he completely demolishes the benefits of any organization - whether that manager represents the board, an administrator, director of resident care or a unit manager.

The responsibility to ensure a supportive and effective organization lies with management and not with staff. Staff can only react to what management initiates.

THE ROLE OF THE MANAGER

"To Be or Not To Be?"

The nurse manager role in long term care is one that has undergone considerable change and development. In the early 1970's the responsibility of nursing in general, and the nurse manager specifically, was limited and clearly defined. Nursing took on a linear role, responsible for direct care and little else. The nursing supervisor in those days had few management demands - her responsibilities mainly involved the day-to-day concerns of direct resident care - medication, treatments, doctor's orders, staff assignments, staff replacing, etc. The director of nursing at that time was often considered the sole manager in the department and was only given responsibility over issues that concerned nursing. In those days many directors of nursing were required to wear a uniform daily and accompany the doctor's on rounds each day.

These positions have changed dramatically in recent years. The nursing supervisor has now become the unit manager. In many facilities her day-to-day nursing responsibilities have been delegated to other nursing staff under her charge - RNA or LPN doing medications and treatments, possibly even another RN responsible for doctors orders and specific care issues. The unit manager is now responsible for management of direct line staff - motivating, directing, educating, disciplining and so on. Organizations have found that the increasing demands of our changing clientele requires a skilled manager to assist staff to meet the increasing demands placed on them.

Likewise, the role of the director of nursing has changed. She has now become the director of resident care. This is a position on the organizational chart that has broadened in its scope to involve all areas concerning resident care. The director of resident care has become responsible for all resident issues regardless of the department involved. This lineal authority, that transcends all boundaries in the organization, represents coordination of the organization as a whole in dealing with quality of life issues for the residents. This new position has increased the scope of responsibilities of the DON to include more involvement in overall organizational budgetary issues, expansion plans, community involvement and concerns, family and board issues, interdepartmental relationships, etc.

Here lies the substantial difference between the nurse manager and managers of other departments. The position of administrator and department heads has been fairly stable, even though the focus of long term care and its clientele has changed. Even though the demands on those managers have increased, the scope of responsibilities have been consistent. It is the nurse manager, whether the unit manager or the director of resident care, who has undergone a significant change in what is expected and what is to be undertaken to fulfill the newly defined role.

Grappling with this changing management role, the nurse managers in long term care have expressed many common complaints and concerns. They are:

"I'm not a manager"

"I don't like managing"

"I didn't plan to be a manager"

"I was never trained to manage"

"I have more to do than just manage"

"I don't know how they want us to manage"

1) "I am not a Manager!"

Some have said "I'm not a manager, that's not my responsibility. I am responsible only for resident care." There is a hesitancy by some nurses to manage, falsely believing that their role does not or should not have any direct responsibility over budgetary issues, cost effectiveness and organizational efficiency. There is confusion about resident care and managing as though they were opposing issues.

Direct budgetary concerns, cost effectiveness and organizational efficiency may not be the nurse manager's first love, but they are definitely interwoven into the equation. The basis for all nurses managing any unit are the standards for nursing practice. Simply put, the nurse manager, whether unionized or not, is responsible for the residents under his/her charge. She is not required to perform the direct care for the forty or fifty residents living on the unit, but she is responsible to ensure that care is delivered by the staff assigned to her.

The nurse manager must use the standards of nursing practice as the criteria to manage her staff. Those standards outline the requirements to ensure a safe resident environment that continually attempts to maximize the residents' abilities, constantly striving to assist those under her care to reach their potential level of independence and, hence, quality of life. Of course, as these standards are enforced, they result in an efficient care team which creates organizational cost effectiveness.

Any nurse in long term care who does not adhere to the established nursing standards is not only an incompetent nurse, but ineffective manager as well. Our nursing responsibility is to ensure the resident's well being in a safe environment. That being the case, there can be few staff and organizational issues that are not the direct responsibility of the nurse manager. There is no difference between a staff member lifting a resident in an unsafe manner to a staff member being late for work. Each scenario creates an unsafe situation. Once the nurse is assigned a unit, she is required to employ effective management skills along with nursing skills to fulfill her responsibilities as a competent registered nurse.

2) "I don't like managing"

One of the common responses by many nurses is "I don't like managing. I don't like disciplining people all of the time." Obviously such an individual has a misconception of what managing is. There is no dispute that years ago, authoritarian management, or managing with a "two-by-four" was the norm. However, in today's style of participatory management, there is little room for the autocrat.

Disciplining is not the main function of management. As a front line manager, if more than a very small percent of your time is disciplining, then you are doing something wrong. Management is a skill that enables one to work with a group of people in providing the needed direction and motivation to achieve a common goal. It is to get staff excited about what they do and where they do it, to ensure that they have the skills, confidence and supports to do their job well.

Probably the worst title that could have been applied to front line managers in long term care is "nursing supervisor." YOU ARE NOT A SUPERVISOR. A foreman on an assembly line may be a supervisor. A supervisor is an individual with a limited number of staff who is responsible for a specific area. Such a supervisor can usually walk up and down the line checking what staff are doing (bolts on tight, etc.) and solve problems as they arise.

How many staff do you have on a unit at one time? On some units it could be six or eight. Along with your other duties, I want you to follow each of your staff the entire eight hours and monitor what they are doing. It is impossible. When you are in one room with one staff member, you do not know what the other five staff are doing down the hall. Most nurse managers in long term care are *working managers*. As we will demonstrate, unlike most management positions, you do much more than just supervise staff. In our setting, the EFFECTIVE MANAGER needs to ensure that staff are self-managed. Those are staff who have been primed by the organization to develop a personal philosophy that ensures their job is completed to the best of their ability.

3) "I didn't plan to be a manager"

This is probably one of the most common circumstances which creates a hesitancy by some nurses to assume fully their management role. How many nurses went into training with the intention of managing a unit? Most entered the profession to provide patient care. We never thought of managing. Often we fell into the position. This creates for some a significant conflict - they would rather do resident care than manage staff. The manager who IS MANAGED usually feels more comfortable dispensing medications, doing treatments, having direct hands on care with the residents, than directing her staff, dealing with staff problems, enhancing communication, etc. The manager who MUST MANAGE takes total responsibility for her residents and does the care through the staff. She does not trust that any of the direct care staff are capable of working independently, without specific direction from her, and treats staff as though they are technicians who are expected only to take orders.

4) "I was never trained to manage"

Were you trained to be a manager? If your position is director of resident care then your response is probably "yes." A unit manager on the other hand will usually answer "no."

In fact, many department heads (housekeeping, maintenance, dietary, etc.) are not trained managers. Instead they were individuals who were good at their jobs, and were promoted to run the department. For the nurse manager in long term care it is a common problem. A registered nurse is trained in providing bedside care, not in managing people. Without proper training and direction any manager is left to perform his job with only the existing skills he may have. This is like asking a person without any training to complete the duties of a registered nurse. Impossible!

5) "I have more to do than manage"

A major problem confronting most nurse managers is that they are *working managers*. Your job is more than dealing with staff and care issues. To demonstrate that, complete the following:

List all of the duties, responsibilities and tasks of the unit or nurse manager (include resident, family, staff, organizational and care issues).

In some facilities that list can be lengthy - health nurse, counselor (family, staff, residents), medications, treatments, answering phone, doctors' rounds, doctors' orders, medication orders, transcribing notes, accident reports (resident and staff), filling pharmacy requisitions, stock requisitions, charting, meetings, emergencies, shift reports, admissions/ discharges/transfers, contact with doctor, making appointments, replacing sick staff - you have probably added many that I have missed.

When do you have time for your staff? It probably wasn't even on your list. Unless the facility in which you work has defined the nurse manager's role and how it is integrated into your job, it can become secondary. Once the task of managing is only added on to other duties, the organization moves from problem solving to crisis intervention. When things cannot be dealt with on the unit as they arise, they are allowed to build until they escalate into a major problem requiring considerable time and energies at all levels of management to resolve. Managing is a role that requires time along with skills. If you don't allocate the time, effective management cannot occur.

6) "I don't know how they want us to manage"

If no one defines what the manager must do - what is acceptable and what is not - then most will eventually do nothing. In a facility that does not provide its managers with direction or guidelines, the manager is left to respond by the "seat of his pants." The problem is one's seat can wear pretty thin. What commonly occurs in such a setting is a trial and error approach to management - try something that you think is right. If it works, no problem. If it doesn't work, look out. When there is no direction to managers on what is expected, they can only evaluate their performance after-the-fact. The manager finds that she does what she believes is best and then is condemned afterwards if it didn't work or wasn't acceptable. Without clearly defined management responsibilities and performance criteria, the manager's actions and the consequences of her behavior are constantly questioned and corrected as to what "should have" been done. If there is no recording of the appropriate and acceptable manner in which a situation should be handled, then at a later date another manager will invariably run into the same problem and experience the same consequences. Such an organization wears its managers down by dealing with the symptoms of its problems and never the problems.

THE ROLE IS CHANGING

When our focus in long term care was mainly custodial - keep them dry, dressed and up - how the manager functioned was not a crucial factor that influenced the results of that care. In those days we told staff what to do and they did it. It was easy. We set the exact time that each bath was to be done, beds made, breaks taken and so on. We could easily measure the success of our care by walking around and counting how many residents were dry, dressed and up and how many were not.

Now the job is more sophisticated. We deal with harder to measure issues involving quality of life for our residents. Physical care has become only one component of the role. Staff are now responsible to meet resident needs on the social, psychological, emotional, behavioral and environmental levels. What the manager does now can dramatically influence the ability of staff to function.

The manager's role in long term care has changed. It now involves encouraging staff to be self-managed. This is a process that imposes on staff certain responsibilities to assess not only their residents, but their jobs as well. It is a need for staff to function independently in determining what they must do with each resident on a daily basis; how to utilize the resources available to encourage resident independence; how to adjust their care and routines to the needs and demands of a wide range of resident functioning abilities; how to integrate into their care the components needed to enhance quality of life; and so on. What it means is that staff are encouraged to think for themselves. Without staff assuming such responsibility, they cannot be responsible.

Yet there are some organizations and managers who are still afraid to take risks. They have a belief that they must constantly regiment their staff, dictating what has to be done and when. Their fear is based on the presence of the negative staff. Those who will abuse any freedoms or flexibility's provided. In order to keep the few staff who may take advantage of an open, self-directing environment, these organizations treat all staff the same - as though all staff are negative.

Limiting all staff in their freedom to be self-managed due to a fear of only a few, inadvertently reinforces the negative. What the organization is saying to all of its staff is - "Whether you are our best staff or not, we are going to treat you as though you are not." If I have no control in the quality of my work or in the use of my time, then I can only assume that my employer does not value my ability to think or believes that I have little of value to contribute. This can only result in my deciding that my worth in the facility is minimal. Once staff develop such an attitude, they will take no ownership in what they do. Such a situation guarantees a low staff morale. Whenever staff morale drops, quality of care soon follows.

When discussing effective management techniques, there are two areas where we must focus our attention - staff supports and defining the manager's role. Both are dependent on each other. Appropriate staff supports assist the manager in effective problem solving and enhancing the organization's functioning ability, and a clearly defined manager's role augments the ability of the staff to perform their duties.

An EFFECTIVE MANAGER treats all of his employees as entrepreneurs, constantly encouraging staff to *own* what they do. Once you have ownership, you have commitment, and with commitment you have responsibility and a well-functioning team to meet the organizational goals. With effective staff supports, the organization enhances staff morale. It excites its staff.

Positive staff morale can be demonstrated when staff can say:
That no matter my role, position or how much time I work:

> *I believe that what I do is important.*
> *What I say is heard.*
> *What I accomplish is recognized.*

If the opposite exists there is no way to excite staff. The outcome can be devastating if staff believe "I'm just a cog-in-the-wheel. It doesn't matter what I do. It doesn't have any meaning or impact." If staff believe that what they do isn't important, then why do it well. There is no incentive to strive for quality.

If staff believe that what they say is never heard, the organization has encouraged "bitching." When staff believe that managers do not want to hear about their concerns or suggestions, or there is no mechanism to encourage staff to share that information, then what do they do with it? They can only communicate their problems laterally. Continually talking about "them" at the coffee table with the belief that there is little they can do to change "them." Talking about problems with no solution in sight, will only reinforce the negative and frustrate the positive.

Finally, if what is accomplished is never recognized, there is no way to motivate staff. Why do direct line staff do what they do? They care about the people in our facilities. It is emotion that drives them. Without recognition to fuel that emotion, there is no way to keep them excited. Without excitement for what they do and where they do it, there is no way they will strive to make a positive difference in the lives of those under their care.

Likewise an organization must respect the manager's morale. That can be demonstrated when a manager can say:

> *As a manager, I know what is expected of me.*
> *I am backed in what I say.*
> *I am supported in what I do.*

To determine your organization's commitment to positive staff and manager morale, complete the following exercise entitled the Staff Needs Assessment.

STAFF NEEDS ASSESSMENT

When we speak of long term care facilities we more often center our attention on the residents and achieving for those residents the highest quality of care. In establishing that goal we cannot overlook one very important link, THE CAREGIVERS. It is no simple task to meet the needs of a wide range of individuals and at the same time provide the highest level of personalized care. To be a caregiver, from administrator to supervisor to nurse's aid to housekeeper, is to be an individual who is constantly in an intense emotional interaction and who finds himself/ herself constantly giving. This is draining and requires an organization that is supportive. Adequate equipment and an appropriate work environment are essential in any organization. But a people facility, a caring facility requires more depth in its provision for its staff. The adage that the quality of care of any facility is only as good as the facility's ability to care for its staff, rings true. The degree of concentration in the area of staff recognition, motivation, support, communication and training is reflected in the level of care given to the residents of that facility.

Saying to a facility "This is what you need to do, therefore do it!" is unrealistic. Each facility is as individualized as the residents and staff within. What is necessary to ensure quality of care is to ensure a growth environment. The complexity of an organization requires an outlook that does not say "This is what should be done!," but "This is what we need to do next!" You and I separately cannot give prolonged quality care. You and I as a team can. We as a team must also ensure that the environment we work in examines our needs, our strengths and weaknesses. Once determined, we can decide on which option fits us. Only then can we formulate a plan to ensure that the environment meets not only the physical needs of both staff and residents, but the personal needs as well.

USE THE FOLLOWING EXERCISE AS A MECHANISM TO IDENTIFY YOUR ORGANIZATION'S STRENGTHS AND WEAKNESSES IN PROVIDING STAFF SUPPORTS.

STAFF NEEDS ASSESSMENT EXERCISE

Next to each of the following statements check either:

#1 **Strong** - what you have in place is working to your liking.

#2 **Weak** - what you have in place is not working to your liking.

#3 **Nonexistent** - there is nothing in place that would satisfy this statement.

Resident Care

1 2 3

1. Work Environment
   __ __ __   - the building is conducive to staff carrying out their duties and performing resident care with the utmost ease (e.g. distance covered from one end of the unit to other, location of store rooms, etc.).

2. Adequate Equipment
   __ __ __   - Staff have sufficient amounts and type of equipment necessary to perform their job.
   __ __ __   - Specialized tools are available for staff to perform care on the heavier care residents (e.g. lifts, elevated chairs, etc.).
   __ __ __   - Resident self help equipment is available, used and encouraged to allow residents to achieve their maximum level of functioning and independence.

3. Comprehension
   __ __ __   - Through training, team meetings, etc. staff receive the information and knowledge needed to understand the relationship between the individual resident, the aging process, disability and the effects of institutionalization.

4. Support Services
   __ __ __   - Staff have access to other professionals (e.g. psychiatrists, physiotherapists, social workers, etc.) to assist in understanding certain residents and determining specific approaches in care.

5. Team Conferences
   __ __ __   - Staff are provided with a mechanism of regularly discussing individual residents to understand their specific behaviors and the rationale for the care established.

6. Input On Work Assignments
___ ___ ___
 - Line staff determine or are part of determining workload assignments on a regular basis, so that work can be equally distributed.

7. Support
___ ___ ___
 - There is an expressed belief that staff are "human" and may not be able to cope or understand all resident behavior.
___ ___ ___
 - There is a mechanism in place to assist staff in that circumstance to receive peer and facility support and the training needed to overcome any difficulties experienced.

8. Relief
___ ___ ___
 - In keeping with the belief that staff are "only human," each staff member has the potential of having a "bad day" or reaching their limit with a specific resident or situation.
___ ___ ___
 - To compensate for this, it is professed, and staff are aware of flexibility in breaks (sit and have a coffee to gather composure) and flexibility in assignments (avoid temporarily being assigned a specific duty or resident that is instigating the problem).

Recognition/Motivation

1 2 3

1. Written Recognition
___ ___ ___
 - Staff/units receive written memos from management on a job well done.
___ ___ ___
 - When letters are received from outside the facility (family, volunteers, etc.) complimenting specific individuals or a specific unit or the facility itself, copies are posted throughout the facility.

2. Outstanding Contributions
___ ___ ___
 - Staff who perform "over-and-above the call of duty" are identified and told of the significance of their contribution.

3. Initial Recognition

___ ___ ___ - Newly hired employees are made to feel welcome and a part of the team by providing a gift or a letter of welcome when they commence their duties.

4. Staff of the Month

___ ___ ___ - There is a mechanism available to the residents of each unit to show their appreciation to specific staff.

5. Staff Environment

___ ___ ___ - There is an area(s) where staff can be away from their work environment during breaks.

6. Verbal Recognition

___ ___ ___ - Management and staff are encouraged and taught to give verbal praise and it is an integral part of the team process.

7. Accreditation

___ ___ ___ - It is sought or has been undertaken and the process well publicized to staff regarding its significance, what it says about the staff and the organization's performance and care.

8. Social Activities

___ ___ ___ - A variety of staff social activities are available on an on-going basis regardless of the number of staff who attend.

9. Master Schedule

___ ___ ___ - A work schedule is in place where all staff know when they are working well in advance of the weekly schedule being posted (with the exception of part time and casual staff).

___ ___ ___ - There is a mechanism where staff have a means of adjusting their schedule as needed.

___ ___ ___ - There are available a number of regular shift postings, including afternoon and nights, that staff can assume for a specific period of time.

10. Consistency in Discipline

__ __ __   - Staff know what to expect and it is enforced regardless of the shift, day or who is on.

11. Management Contact

__ __ __   - All levels of management are seen on each unit on a regular basis each week.

__ __ __   - Management staff are involved in certain resident activities where staff are expected to participate.

12. Stress Days

__ __ __   - All levels of staff have the opportunity to attend outside workshops/seminars. This is encouraged by providing days off work with pay or flexibility in re-arranging work schedules or payment of registration fees.

13. LOA Without Pay

__ __ __   - All staff are aware that a leave of absence without pay may be granted on request as long as adequate notice is given and the request does not conflict with established peak holiday periods.

14. Counseling (Formal & Informal)

__ __ __   - Formal - the facility has made arrangements with local counseling agencies (e.g. marital, substance abuse, financial, etc.) to be able to refer staff when a specific personal problem or difficulty is identified.

__ __ __   - Informal - all management staff are provided with some training in counseling skills.

15. Support Group

__ __ __   - Staff are encouraged to "get together" in order to strengthen relationships, discuss problems and solutions, air differences, gain an understanding of each other's perspective (e.g. intermingling during breaks, staff dinners, in-service sessions, educational days, etc.).

COMMUNICATION

1 2 3

1. Meetings (Unit & Facility)
   - Staff are encouraged to attend regular meetings that allow them to identify and resolve problems experienced on their unit, within their department and regarding the facility in general.

2. Memos + System for Attention
   - Memos are used regularly (not abused) and are brief and to the point.
   - There is a mechanism that ensures that all staff are aware of memos sent to their attention.

3. Suggestion Box
   - These are available throughout the facility and there is a mechanism of communicating to staff the answer to each suggestion submitted.

4. Staff Newsletter
   - There is a mechanism where staff on all shifts, whether part time, full time or casual can learn what is happening, what is changing and what is coming up.

5. Participatory Decision Making
   - Staff have input and are encouraged to be involved in any decisions related to their job (within reason).
   - There is both a formal and informal mechanism in place that allows staff to know of the decision being considered and to communicate their questions and recommendations regardless of the issue at hand.

6. Performance Appraisal
   - Performed on a regular basis, each staff member is provided with an opportunity to know how he/she is doing.

7. Goal Flow Chart

___ ___ ___   - All staff know what is happening on their unit or in the facility in regards to change, additions, renovations, etc. 6 months to 2 years in advance (where possible).

8. Brainstorming Sessions

___ ___ ___   - Representatives of all departments and all levels of staff are brought together on a yearly basis to discuss as a group the problems and shortcomings, strengths and weaknesses of the facility, as well as making recommendations for possible solutions or changes they can see being implemented.

9. Strategic Planning Sessions

___ ___ ___   - "Hot spots" in the facility, unit, department or shift are provided with the opportunity to meet with managers to air their feelings regarding their situation.

10. Informal Discussions

___ ___ ___   - Staff have the opportunity to meet with different management levels at specific times to discuss issues informally (e.g. specific management staff will be available in a certain location every second Tuesday of the month during lunch for any staff who would like to meet).

SUMMARY

It is one thing for you as the manager to complete this questionnaire. How would your staff complete it?

Management may believe that certain staff supports are in place only to find that their staff are not aware of them. If what we profess and do as managers is not clearly defined or consistently implemented, then it is of no value. I encourage you to have some of your staff complete this questionnaire and then compare their responses to yours. Not only will you be able to identify the strengths and weaknesses within your facility, you will also have an opportunity to rectify some of the misconceptions and misunderstandings held by both groups.

We have just completed the first segment of this text - identifying the problems. At this point we have examined:

⇒ the variety of problems that can be experienced by any organization (psychological, communicational, organizational, interpersonal and personal)

⇒ the characteristics specific to long term care facilities

⇒ three management types (the EFFECTIVE MANAGER, the manager who IS MANAGED and the manager who MUST MANAGE) and management dynamics

⇒ three staff performance groups (positive, average and negative) and staffing dynamics

⇒ organizational dynamics and the effects of negative staff and the managers who MUST MANAGE

⇒ an outline of the managers role within our setting

⇒ an overview of the supports required by managers and staff to do their job effectively.

All of the discussion to this point has centered around management and organizational problems. The following chapters will present specific interventions needed to rectify those problems.

The play is unfolding.
Our characters have all appeared.
The plot has been presented.
It is now time to unravel the mystery.

Chapter Six

ON BECOMING AN EFFECTIVE MANAGER

Take time to answer the following question. Jot down your answer in the space provided or lift your eyes from the page for a moment to consider your response:

What are the qualities that make a person successful?.

Generally the qualities identified in answering this question are varied, extensive and highly impressive. Unfortunately you will probably never meet a person who possesses all of those qualities. The belief by some that you have to be someone special, someone fortunate or someone gifted to be successful is unfounded. There are a number of very successful people who excel in only a few personal qualities. Those qualities are:

a) Excitement - They have an enthusiasm for what they are doing and what they strive for that is noticed by everyone. In their presence you cannot help but be caught up by their excitement as they talk about their objective.

b) Drive - This is a person who is intent on achieving something that fuels that excitement. All of his energies are focused on that specific outcome. He will not allow anything to deflect him from that goal.

c) <u>Determination</u> - Lastly the successful person knows that achieving his goal will not be easy. Even though things are encountered that may temporarily block him, he is always looking for a solution. Never allowing anything to decrease his enthusiasm.

It is common for many to believe that they do not have the qualities to be successful. That perception is inaccurate. Please answer the following questions.

> *How did you feel when you first started the job you presently have?*
> *How strong was your excitement the first few days/weeks/months?*
> *Your drive?*
> *Your determination to make change?*

I guarantee that everyone is highly motivated when they begin a new job. Now to the next question.

> *How do you feel about your job now?*
> *How strong is your excitement?*
> *Your drive?*
> *Your determination to make change?*

If you have lost any of those feelings, imagine how successful you would be if you had the same excitement, drive and determination as you did those first few days. The reality is that anyone can be successful.

THE VIEW OF OTHERS

Let me now share with you the difference between those who will always be successful and those who will never be successful. The person who will always be successful keeps talking about what he can do. The person who will never be successful only talks about what he can't do. This may seem too simplistic. Yet it is the key component that differentiates these two outcomes.

As we have demonstrated in the discussion of management dynamics and staff profiles, there are individuals who have developed in themselves an apathy or negativity that has the ability to influence others. They utter *comments that are meant to paralyze.* How many times have you heard these and probably many more from those around you?

> *It is unrealistic.*
> *No one cares.*
> *There isn't enough money, staff, equipment, time, etc., etc..*
> *We tried that 10 years ago. It didn't work then, it won't work*
>   *now.*
> *Yes, but . . . (complete this any way you'd like, there are*
>   *numerous conclusions to this statement.)*
> *No one will support us.*
> *You can't trust them to follow through.*
> *It can't be done.*
> *There is no one to do it.*
> *No one will listen.*
> *It won't happen.*

Those who mutter this credo have very unique characteristics. These people fear anything that involves risk. They are satisfied with the status quo, even though they do not enjoy or are frustrated by the status quo. They know that for the status quo to be different requires them to change the things that maintain it. The unsuccessful person's perception of change, or anything new or different is that it will only fail. These people can be called AVOIDERS. They invest most of their energy to avoid anything that may initiate their fears. They openly *resist* change or the efforts of others to implement change.

Then there are those who strive for change. They see growth as a challenge, something positive, needed and exciting. For these people a challenge makes the job worthwhile and rewarding. They can be called INITIATORS. They are always focused on the end result or outcome. They will *persist* at whatever it is they are attempting to do, until it is done.

We have just identified one of the major organizational conflicts that can occur. The Avoiders and Initiators are at loggerheads. Their values, actions and desires are at opposing ends to the other. Let us now identify the management styles and staffing profiles as they apply to these qualities.

Initiator - The obvious two who fit this classification are the EFFECTIVE MANAGER and the positive staff.

Avoider - These are the Negative staff and the manager who MUST MANAGE. The negative staff are apparent. These people believe that everything will fail, therefore why try. To them anything new or different is a waste of time or energy. For this person everything is too difficult, too hard, too much time, too much effort, too . . , too . . . The manager who MUST MANAGE also qualifies as an Avoider. This individual is not a risk taker. He does not trust others. He believes the only way anything can be done well is for him to do it. His need to be in control constantly *resists* the involvement and efforts of others.

Follower - There are two groups who are neither Avoiders or Initiators, but Followers. These people neither persist or resist, but simply *follow* the path of least resistance. They are the average staff who will follow whoever is the most powerful and the manager who IS MANAGED is influenced by his conflict avoidance behavior. Neither of these will take a stand either way.

Which are you - an Avoider, Follower or Initiator?

TAKING A STAND

Philosophies and principles of care are easy to profess. In my seminars, many nod their heads in agreement to what is being proposed about resident care and quality of life, indicating that it is what they believe and follow. Unfortunately, when some return to their workplace and are confronted by an ineffective manager, negative staff or even limited resources, they take those philosophies and principles of care and throw them out the window. It is easy to profess who you are and what you believe in when things are going well. You only know what you stand for when you are <u>challenged</u>.

Return to the list of *comments that are meant to paralyze.*

> *Which one response, comment, rejection is enough to shut you down?*

There is absolutely no problem that does not have a solution. Unfortunately, there is no solution that can be implemented until someone becomes excited about it, driven to achieve it and determined to make it happen regardless of what is encountered.

The most common block to any solution is when we allow the Avoiders to be successful. The Avoider always attempts to stifle the creativity and excitement of an Initiator. They are successful when they can change Initiators. Converting an excited, driven and determined Initiator into a Follower or even another Avoider. Back to the list of *comments meant to paralyze.*

> *How many times have **you** spoken these comments to others about their ideas?*
> *How many times have **you** spoken these comments to yourself about your own ideas?*
> *How many times do **you** stop yourself even before others try?*

It is not the action of others, but the inaction of ourselves that prevents our being successful. The Avoider is successful when the Initiator finally *creates limits for himself even before limits are created by others.*

As a manager, just as a nurse, you are guaranteed of experiencing one thing in your job - problems. When encountering a problem, you have only two options available - to allow that problem to paralyze you or to find a solution. Allowing a problem to paralyze you gives that event the power to define who you are. Finding a solution on the other hand gives you the power. The decision of what you do with each problem encountered is yours.

How Confident are You in You?

How much power are you willing to give others to decide who you are?

This question can best be answered by a simple example. During nurse's training years ago, I remember a 19 year old classmate who was a natural leader. Her assertiveness and problem solving skills were evident to all. Anyone she contacted was always influenced by her excitement, drive and determination.

A few years ago while I was on a speaking tour, she attended one of my seminars scheduled in her area. During the first coffee break she approached me and asked if I remembered her. I couldn't place her (a few years had passed since our training days). She then told me her maiden name. As soon as I heard it I identified her immediately. As we talked, she asked if I remembered how she was during those earlier days. I said "Who could forget? You impressed everyone." She responded "I am not like that anymore." That took me by surprise and I had to ask "What changed?" She stated "A few years ago I had this boss who burned me bad because I was open and direct about a certain issue. I learned never to do that again."

Isn't that amazing! She allowed one person and one event to strip her of the qualities that made her who she was. That is giving away power.

There is a common question I ask during one of my seminars on stress management. I need to ask you that question now.

In your personal or professional life, *who is in the driver's seat*?
You?
Or the people or events in your life?

It is time now for you to make a decision.

If you have lost the feelings you had in the first few days of starting your job, what *do you need to do* to gain them back?

It is obvious by now that this text is not only about your organization, but it is about you. None of the interventions or strategies discussed in the upcoming pages can be implemented without you. They require you to be excited again. To have drive. To be determined. For *you* to be ***successful***.

USING THE SKILLS YOU HAVE

Being successful within an organization requires the ability to adapt to the personalities of those within that setting. To achieve that goal you must tap one of your most powerful skills as a professional caregiver. You are a people reader. You have the ability to constantly adapt your approach to fit the personality and characteristics of each client you encounter. Let me demonstrate.

You know that approaching certain residents and saying "It is time to go to an activity" will only result in their not going. The personality of some residents dictates that they must always be in control. This individual does not accept anything that he can interpret as a command. On hearing a command, he will *resist* going to the activity even though he may want to attend. Approaching that same resident and stating "There is an activity scheduled. What about seeing if it is worthwhile?" will probably have a greater chance of success.

Likewise, approaching other residents with that same open ended question will probably result in their not attending. Some individuals are more passive. They have the tendency to be a *follower*, taking the direction of others. If no direction is defined, then no action is taken. The only successful way to have this resident attend an activity is to be more direct and assertive, "I think you should go to the activity." With this comment he will more probably attend.

By the way, utilizing the same strategies you employ for the resident who must be in control and the resident who is passive will enhance your success with your managers.

To be successful with the manager who MUST MANAGE, you need to allow that person to feel that he is in control. To be successful with the manager who IS MANAGED, you must take control.

The same holds true in dealing with negative staff. Apply the same skills you employ with the negative resident. When a resident is always critical about what you do, his care and where he lives, you do not agree with his assessment and abandon caring for him. Instead you approach him in a way that contradicts his perception. You learn to anticipate his response so that you can maintain objectivity with each encounter; to always assist him to find a solution to what bothers him; and to consistently talk in the positive to challenge him to see things in a different light. You *persist* to ensure that you are successful in the delivery of your care.

We have demonstrated that the skills that make you a successful professional caregiver, are the skills that make you a successful manager. It is your ability to assess an individual's perception and then adapt your approach to that person that ensures success in achieving your desired outcome. Employing those same skills in an organization means moving from a passive or defensive role - waiting for the ineffective individual to take action - to an assertive role - your ensuring that action is taken. The ultimate result is that you will be able to avoid being controlled by those around you who are ineffective - negative staff, the manager who MUST MANAGE and the manager who IS MANAGED.

LEARNING TO MANAGE YOUR MANAGER

TAKING THE ASSERTIVE ROLE

To avoid being controlled by an individual who is ineffective, one must learn to be assertive. In dealing with either the manager who IS MANAGED or the manager who MUST MANAGE, you cannot wait until that person has time to deal with the issues that concerns you. With the manager who IS MANAGED that time will probably never arrive. A survival technique by this management style is to implement a consist philosophy of - "I'll get around to it." By avoiding issues, he attempts to avoid the need to take action. Inaction avoids conflict. The result is he never gets "around to it."

The manager who MUST MANAGE, on the other hand will get around to it when it becomes his priority. Unfortunately, his sense of what is priority may not agree with yours. Remember he assesses situations based on how he perceives them, not how they really are. If he does not place your concern or problem as a priority, then you can wait for some time before it is addressed. Either management style has the potential of hampering your effectiveness and dampening your excitement.

Instead of waiting for direction, *define the direction*. Assume an assertive posture. There are a number of strategies that will allow you to achieve the desired success.

WRITTEN COMMUNICATION

After discussing any issue, send your manager a summary memo. State "My understanding is that you would like *the following* done by *the following* date. If I do not hear from you within two weeks I will proceed on that basis." By this simple strategy, both management styles are placed in the situation of either responding or not responding. No matter the result, some action will be taken.

The manager who MUST MANAGE will get back to you to clarify if he does not agree with what you have presented. If he does not respond to your memo, then his non-response indicates that he has approved for you to proceed as outlined. This gives him the perception that you will be doing what you understood *he wants*. He is still in control. You are moving forward.

The manager who IS MANAGED on the other hand will probably not respond. His non-response is permission to go ahead. Undoubtedly you received permission to do what you wanted when you spoke with him (remember the head nods). Placing in writing what you understood from the meeting and stating that you will implement it by a certain date unless you hear otherwise, is soliciting his approval. It is difficult to withdraw his support in the future if conflict should occur. When handled in this manner, he cannot easily delegate blame to you professing that he did not remember giving you permission.

You have taken control. Established direction. You have succeeded. You are excited.

USING "I" ASSERTION AND ENSURING ACCOUNTABILITY

In any organization there is a simple reality - we all have "bosses." Having someone in authority over you limits your problem solving ability. You may not have the authority to take unilateral action on things like staff or resource shortages, inconsistency in management practices, etc., without discussing it with your manager. In some instances, simply discussing the problem with your manager may be the greatest challenge. The manager who MUST MANAGE may not be willing to discuss the problem because he does not see it as you do, making it a low priority in his schedule right now. The manager who IS MANAGED will always attempt to avoid discussing it.

Discussing certain concerns with your manager may require you to be more direct in order to get his attention. If your manager has directly or indirectly avoided talking about a concern, then still document it in a memo. Request in writing an opportunity to meet with that manager by a specific date to discuss your concern. This simple action can have a significant impact. The Effective Manager will probably see this as a call to action. The manager who MUST MANAGE may be forced to place this into his priority. The manager who IS MANAGED may realize that your documenting a concern requires him to address it. Remember his response to the written grievance. You have created for him a potential conflict in the similar manner.

Ensure that the memo is written in a <u>positive</u> and <u>objective</u> manner. Imagine if the memo were sent to you and written with the following comments - "*You* do not understand . . . *You* have not dealt with . . . *You* have had this brought to your attention before and *you* did nothing about it." What would be your reaction to these statements? You would probably interpret them as being accusatory. Using the word *you* during any communication - verbal or written - can place the other person in a defensive mode. Instead of focusing on the issue, the individual will be forced to focus on the words used and what they may imply. You are now off topic. The opportunity to deal with the issue is lost.

One of the most effective ways to communicate to anyone is to use the technique of "*I*" assertion. This ensures a positive and objective interaction. The technique is a simple one, but it takes some practice to master. It involves talking not in the *you* but in the "*I*." For example - "*I*

127

have been frustrated by . . . *I* do not understand the direction that needs to be taken. *I* would like the opportunity to discuss this so that *I* can have it clarified." In this way the other person is drawn into the issue. This technique requests assistance, rather than solicits the resistance of that person. Objectivity is better ensured. You have taken responsibility for the task at hand.

Remember that the content of your memo must be objective and positive. The goal is to find a solution, not to prove the other person wrong or inept. If you have been frustrated with your job, what may seem positive and objective to you, may not appear the same to others. Your emotions can easily cloud your objectivity. To counter this, it is valuable to give the memo to someone who has nothing to do with your organization before sending it to your manager. You may be surprised by that person's critique - "You are going to say that?" In this way you can be ensured that your frustration does not spill into the memo and impede your success.

When you send a copy of the memo to your manager, keep a copy for yourself. If the manager does not respond by the defined date, then send a reminder memo - "*I* was hoping to discuss that issue with you. *I* still have some concerns. *I* would like to meet by . . ." Set another date.

Even with these memos and utilizing the "I" assertion technique, you are not guaranteed that the issue will be discussed, let alone resolved. Remember that some ineffective managers have learned skills that may make them highly successful at being ineffective no matter what they encounter. These memos and the "I" assertion technique ensures that accountability is in the hands of the person who has the authority to deal with it. Should the problem erupt into something more serious, your manager cannot say - "I didn't know about it" or "You didn't tell me it was that important." Your memos ensures that you will not be held accountable for the consequences of a problem simply because your manager is unwilling to deal with it. You have just managed your manager.

By the way, the organization as a whole can utilize this same strategy at another level. There are issues that the entire management team may not be able to resolve without direction or support from the government agency controlling those resources (i.e. finances or staffing levels). A memo needs to be sent to that government agency identifying the concern, asking for their assistance by a certain date. They will either be compelled to send in a representative to assist in finding a solution or will not take action. In either case, it will be addressed. If serious problems erupt because it was not resolved, then accountability can be directed to those who had the authority to deal with it.

ASSERTIVENESS AND THE NEGATIVE STAFF

It is important to take this opportunity to deal with the actions of negative staff as well. The chronic "bitcher" sees fault in anything and everything. To be effective with this individual is to use the same strategies you employ with the negative resident. Anticipate this staff member's response so that you can maintain objectivity with each encounter; always assist him to find a solution to what bothers him; and consistently talk in the positive to challenge him to see things in a different light.

Anticipating this staff member's response allows you to be in control of the situation, not to be controlled by it. This staff member on *every* contact will constantly lament - "This place stinks . They don't listen." If you do not anticipate these comments in advance you can easily be caught up in the "bitching" or tend to avoid the individual.

Recall the topic discussed on psychological game playing in chapter two. The negative staff will only initiate the bitching when the opportunity allows itself. This person will usually target other individuals who have become frustrated or lost their excitement. It is when you are "off guard" and "low" that you are the most vulnerable to the negative staff. You can be drawn into the "bitching." When a positive staff member or any manager is drawn into the "bitching," it reinforces this person's belief system. You have agreed with this person's perception of the situation. This gives the individual a feeling of power and provides a source of recognition. When you learn to anticipate this person's comments and behavior, you are more able to maintain your objectivity and be in control.

The worst thing you can do is to lose control with the negative staff. Losing control can result in your avoiding this individual or being accusatory. If you avoid the person, you can easily be labeled by the negative staff as "one of *them*." When you intentionally sit at another table during coffee break you are now the target - "Look at her. She is too good for us. She won't even sit with us during break."

If you lose control and become accusatory, you lose. To finally respond to this person's constant "bitching" by saying "*Your* negativity drives me crazy. *You* are always talking about things but *you* never do anything about them." You again have given the negative staff the opportunity to make you the target. He can now say to others - "I tried to talk to her about something that was bothering me and she told me off."

There is a simple assertiveness strategy that will allow you to be successful with the negative staff on every occasion. When a negative staff member begins "bitching," respond by saying - "That is a good point how do you think we could resolve it?" That staff member will be off balance and usually respond back with a further negative comment - "*They* don't resolve anything here." or "*They* don't listen to *us*." Stay with that same response - "That is a good problem as well,. How do you think we could resolve that?" In assertiveness, the technique is called "The Broken Record." - staying with your goal regardless of what you encounter. Your goal is to find a solution to what bothers him. Your consistently talking to him in a positive manner challenges him to see things in a different light

I am not suggesting that a negative staff member will suddenly change his perception and always deal with the issue. Let us be honest. Even though a person is always negative, what he is professing may have an element of truth to it. The negative staff member may need some help in weeding through their accusatory comments to uncover the problem that needs to be resolved. Persisting with that straightforward comment may have a surprising effect. He may open up and discuss possible solutions to that problem once it is clearly defined. Or he may not. Either way you will be successful.

Being persistent with that comment will result in the negative staff member beginning to anticipate your actions. This person will soon realize that every time he sits with you and begins "bitching," your response is always "That is a good point. How do you think we could resolve that?" If he is unwilling to deal with the issue, he will probably stop sitting with you. You no longer avoid the person. He avoids you. The comment "How do you think we can resolve it" provides him with no ammunition to make you the target of his "bitching." It is hard to say to others with any degree of credibility "Isn't she a pip. Every time you talk to her about something all she wants to do is solve it."

The latter outcome removes from the "bitcher" an audience. Imagine if the majority of staff and managers in an organization used that statement with every issue that the negative staff presented. The negative staff who were intent on only "bitching" and not resolving problems would soon have no one to "bitch" to. It is hard to "bitch" to a table of empty chairs and still appear rational.

CHANGING PERSPECTIVES - STRIPPING POWER

Do you have a boss or negative employee that seems as though he is ten feet tall and four feet wide?
What happens when you make contact with that person?

All of us have people in our lives who appear to have a dominating power over us. When interacting with this individual, all of our skills in assertiveness and problem solving seem to evaporate. If a boss has such an effect over you, you have experienced the following.

You approach this boss's office to talk to him regarding a concern or make a request. In advance of your meeting you made a concerted effort to prepare for what you want to accomplish. You virtually composed a script within your mind, deciding how you would present your concerns, postulating how your boss may respond and preparing your answers. You rehearsed the dialogue repeatedly to ensure that nothing went wrong. You knock on his door. You hear the response "**YES**." You walk in and stammer out "I uh. . ., I uh . . ., I uh . . . ." Everything you rehearsed just falls apart. You leave the office not accomplishing anything you set out to do, asking yourself as you walk down the hall "What happened?" You know that if this were anyone else, you would be in control of both yourself and the situation to ensure an objective, problem solving discussion, instead of a wishy-washy outcome.

We have people in our lives to whom we give a great deal of power, whether that person is a boss or negative staff member. As easily as we can give that power away, we can take it back.

You would rarely give such power to a resident regardless of his behavior. If a resident yelled "Get out of here and leave me alone" when you tried to give him his medication, you would not turn tail and run. You would deal with the issue and work through his behavior so the necessary task can be completed.

The same approach is needed when dealing with that employee or boss who intimidates or manipulates you. To strip that person of his power, just change your mental picture of what is happening.

> I want you to make a mental image of that person at work who seems to you to be ten feet tall and four feet wide.
> Raise your eyes from the page to create the image.

> Now picture that person in a hospital gown.
> A short hospital gown
> With an open back.
> Again look away from the page to get a clear picture.
> What happens to the picture?

It shrinks in size. When you change the picture, that person's power evaporates. The next time you are in contact with a person who seems to strip you of your power create the same imagery.

> As you stand in front of him.
> Imagine him wearing such a gown.
> Picture what that person's knees would look like.
> His backside.

You will smile but more importantly you will change your response and feel more in control. It is hard for a person to have a lot of power when he is seen in a short, open-backed hospital gown. Remove the power and you even the odds.

The same is true for speaking in front of a group. Some managers find it difficult to talk to a group of people, yet it is an important role for every manager. The same way we gave that boss or negative employee power over us, we give power to a group. There is a simple solution. The next time you present to a group, imagine all of them sitting on the *toilet*. Remarkable how little power a group of people have when they are sitting on a toilet. What you are doing when you undertake this mental exercise is allowing yourself to change the outcome. Your internal smile allows you to break your normal reflex pattern in such a situation and provides you the opportunity to respond in a more controlled and effective manner.

Group - Presentation Technique

While we are on this topic of dealing with groups, there are a few other strategies to enhance your effectiveness. The first is to mentally decrease the numbers you have to face which will elevate your comfort zone. When you are required to make your next presentation, whether to a group of six or sixty people, target only two people in the audience before you begin. Pick one who is sitting in the front and one sitting at the back. During your opening and initial discussion, direct your conversation to those two people only, ignoring the rest of the group. Make an effort to establish eye contact with only those two as if there were no one else in the room. Talking to two is much easier for some than talking to sixty. Once you find yourself becoming comfortable, you will also find your eyes will naturally wander to the rest sitting in the room. Always remember the best way to be sure you are heard by all is to keep telling yourself to speak up because the entire group is hard of hearing.

It is simple when you think of it. It is our mental imagery that creates our problems when interacting with specific people or groups of people. As easy as it is to create that imagery, you can change it, enhancing your effectiveness and confidence.

Communicating Without Communicating

1) Changing Vocabulary and Perception

Our perception of a situation has a powerful influence on our success and excitement. When we believe that the possible solution to a situation is out of reach (too difficult, too much time, too complicated, etc.) then our expectation of a positive resolution is dampened. The word "problem" can have that effect. For some that word implies too difficult a task to find a solution, or worse, implies that it is beyond that person's grasp to resolve and must only be solved by others.

An effective way to counter these dynamics within yourself and your work place is to establish two simple rules -

> a) a "problem" is always referred to as a *challenge*
> b) never come to me with a challenge without a possible
> solution.

When one is confronted with a challenge instead of a problem, perception of it's outcome is changed. A challenge implies that a solution is available. The only task then is to uncover it. That belief elicits excitement. Changing your vocabulary in this fundamental way, will change your perception, which will change your outcome. We have uncovered another quality of the successful person - the ability to create his own excitement.

The second rule has a different effect. When your team members know that they can bring any challenge (problem) to you, as long as they bring a solution, it also defines the expectations you have of them:

> - *their ideas have value*
> - *they are responsible to think*
> - *they are part of the problem solving process.*

With this expectation, you will get your staff excited. Excited about who they are, their role and where they work.

2) Positioning

Managers are required to assume a variety of roles with staff - confidant, counselor, disciplinarian, problem solver, etc.

How do your staff know which role you have taken when they talk with you?

Effective positioning is a skill that can unconsciously communicate your intentions to anyone. To utilize this technique, a manager's office requires five chairs - one behind the desk, two in front and two comfortable chairs located in the corner of the room. When dealing with a disciplinary issue or one where you expect little discussion, position yourself in the chair behind the desk. When problem solving or counseling where you want to encourage open discussion, sit next to the person in one of the two chairs in the corner. Once staff become aware of your pattern, they will respond accordingly. This simple technique can be so effective, that if a staff member walks into your office and finds you sitting behind your desk, she may very well ask if she needs a union steward present.

If you do not have an office, or the office you have is too small for five chairs, then use the location of the chair and its proximity to your desk for the same effect. When you want open discussion, draw your chair to the side of the desk. When you want to assert your role as "boss," sit with the chair located behind your desk. In this way you have decreased the confusion that can be created by the diversity of roles you must assume.

3) Controlling a Meeting

How many times have you read the minutes of a meeting you attended and responded "Where did this come from? I don't remember talking about that." A recorder transcribing the minutes of a meeting on a standard sheet of paper is an inaccurate and time consuming method of summarizing what the group is saying. A flip chart is needed for recording at every meeting for a number of reasons.

⇒ It ensures that what is being written is accurate. Without a flip chart, the recorder writes what he thinks the group is saying, which may be a different perception than what is discussed. Using a flip chart allows the recorder's notes to be visible to the group, providing group members the opportunity to correct any misinterpretations or misunderstandings before they are entered into the minutes.

⇒ Using a flip chart is time saving. As each page on the flip chart is filled, it is then taped to the wall. Participants can refer back to earlier points, add and delete issues as the discussion unfolds without continually asking the recorder to read back what was written.

⇒ Recording on a flip chart keeps people attentive. By stimulating verbal as well as auditory senses, people are more apt to follow the discussion.

⇒ Whoever uses the flip chart will dictate the outcome of the meeting.

This last point is important to the manager. Many staff in a group discussion are conscious of the manager's authority and are reluctant to pursue issues that are evidently not acceptable. Interpreting your non-verbal cueing may become a way to help staff to know what you are thinking about at any point. Reading your actions, facial expressions and movements may assist staff to know whether it is safe to continue with what they are saying or whether they should stop.

Imagine the following:

> *You are the manager chairing a staff meeting. You are also the recorder writing on the flip chart. A staff member presents a suggestion. You stall for a moment and raise your eyebrows, then write what she has said.*

Your hesitation may have a simple reason behind it, but to staff it is a significant cue. To you the suggestion presented may be valid, but you were suddenly aware that it would require you to re-arrange your entire schedule for the week. Regardless of the reasons for your action, that staff member could easily read your behavior and facial expression to mean that this is a delicate topic. Her decision may then be to discontinue the discussion or limit it for fear of treading on delicate ground that you may not approve.

Allowing one of the staff to become the recorder ensures an open discussion. When the manger is not the recorder, he is required to sit with the group and is under less scrutiny by the group members than before. It is very difficult for staff to read your reaction to any one comment if their attention is focused on the recorder. For you to demonstrate your concern about any issue requires you to verbally express them, forcing you to expand your point of view. In this way staff feel less intimidated in their discussion.

CONFRONTING STAFF ISSUES - THE DIRECTIONAL LEVEL

A common response by many nurse managers is - "I don't like managing because I don't like to discipline staff." Managing is not disciplining. In fact if you are spending your time disciplining, then you are probably not managing effectively. Effective managing is providing direction, motivating, and delegating. It is getting people excited, not afraid. There is no question that disciplinary action may be needed at times. That is part of the role, but it is not the only part.

I want you to place this book down for a moment, then pick it up. I know this is a peculiar request of a writer, but please do it anyway.

Now that you have the book back in your hands, there is something I must tell you - "*You* shouldn't have placed the book where *you* put it, *you* should have put it a foot over to the right."

What is your response to my critique of where you placed the book? You are forced to defend your actions. As demonstrated earlier, using the word "*you*" can be interpreted as accusatory and in this instance a criticism of your ability. If that is how issues are approached when dealing with staff, then they can easily be viewed as a reprimand and the objective of resolving the issue lost.

Many managers have experienced confrontations with their staff because of one simple fact - their initial interaction on a certain issue was to accuse before providing the needed direction. Telling you what you did wrong is a demotivator and does not provide you with any direction on how to correct it. Telling you what I expect of your performance ensures success and will have a greater chance of instilling excitement. Let me explain further. In management there are two distinct levels of interaction with staff - Directional and Disciplinary.

Before a staff member can legitimately be corrected on a certain action, the manager must be sure that clear direction of what is expected and its rationale is given. As a manager you may not consider what you are saying as a reprimand, but staff may easily interpret it as so. Remember that with some staff (especially negative staff) what you say and do is always under scrutiny. When a staff member can interpret what you are saying as a criticism, then at that instance that person is unlikely to be listening. He feels forced to defend his actions as you would be forced to do when I accused you of placing your book in the wrong spot.

Back to the example of placing the book down. Imagine if my response were different - "I find it important to place the book one foot to the right to allow those coming on duty easy access to it. If it is not in the same place consistently, others waste considerable time trying to find it." Your probable response would be "OK" or you would comment on why you believe it is important to place the book elsewhere. In either case we are problem solving, dealing with the issue at hand, not with what was said or why you did what you did.

What we are defining is management assertiveness. A process that emphasizes three specific components:

⇒ *Communicating in the "I"*
⇒ *Dealing with an "it"*
⇒ *Talking in the positive*

The effective manager provides direction that centers on a specific issue and keeps personality and emotions separate. It is a process of always communicating to staff what is expected of them. Done effectively, the only response that a staff member can make is to say "Thank you."

An example of how this may be expressed is as follows:

On this unit I (we) expect _____
The reason for that is _____
What will happen if it isn't done is _____

*[Note: Some managers have difficulty using the pronoun "I"
and are more comfortable with "we."]*

Communicating in the "I" is stating that the person's actions effects you, the unit or the organization as a whole. Giving the rationale of what is expected provides the understanding that will motivate the individual to follow through. Likewise, dealing with an "it" or a thing rather than the person keeps it objective. And finally, talking in the positive stresses the solution rather than the action. The outcome is not to criticize what was done, but define what is expected and why.

Let us take a few examples. A staff member has been feeding a resident who is capable of feeding herself. To say "You are not supposed to be feeding that lady," can easily initiate the response "Nobody told me." We have moved now from the issue of feeding a resident, to the belief that staff must be told directly and repeatedly every aspect of the care they perform. That is the purpose of the care plan. Remember the psychological game of "Yes, but . . ." This individual is delegating blame to someone else. Rather than taking ownership for her responsibilities and fulfilling the philosophy of care promoted by the facility, she has placed that onus on others. Do not be swayed from what it is that you believe must be addressed. Use the assertive technique of the "Broken Record." The issue here involves encouraging a resident to be independent and understanding what would occur if that were not done.

The assertive response in this example would be - "On this unit I expect my staff to encourage the resident to be as independent as possible. The reason for that is to enhance the resident's quality of life, allowing him to do for himself as much as possible. When that is not done, the resident becomes more dependent on us, negatively effecting her self image."

In that interaction there is little that can be said in return but "I understand." Later in this chapter we will discuss what the next step should be if that same staff member was discovered feeding the resident again.

Let us take another example. Suppose you were told that a certain staff member was "bitching" to other staff about problems on the unit, but not talking to you about the issues directly. To approach that staff member and say "I heard you were bitching," results in the most obvious response "Who told you that?" To deal with something that is hearsay is to take one person's word over another. A non-accusatory response when someone is suspected of "bitching" is - "On my unit I expect my staff to talk with me when they have a problem. The reason for that is I cannot help solve something I know nothing about. If problems are not solved, then staff will have to be content to live with them." That staff member knows what is expected, whether he was bitching or not.

In each example, you have reinforced your *standards of performance* - the expectations you have of any member of your team. The technique of management assertiveness is simple, but it is not easy. The challenge is to take the "you" out of your conversation when dealing with a specific issue. There is a way to master that skill. Imagine that you are talking to a new employee during his orientation period. With a new employee you would provide the needed direction to understand his role and the rationale behind it. When using this imagery technique while practicing management assertiveness with your staff, you will be more apt to place the issue in the forefront. This will result in your communicating what you expect, why it is needed and the consequences should it not be completed in that manner.

The immediate question initiated by managers is - "How many times do you do this with one staff member?" The answer is simple - *once*. The next step is personal and more direct. If you find the same staff member repeating the same behavior or action that you corrected earlier, then the response is straight forward "I have already explained to you what is expected. You have not followed through. Why is that?" That staff member cannot respond "I didn't know," but instead is required to explain her actions.

For the EFFECTIVE MANAGER this is an easy technique. You do it all the time. To the manager who IS MANAGED or those who MUST MANAGE, it is another matter.

To those who MUST MANAGE, this is a way of toning down the abrupt manner used when interacting with staff. It is a way of breaking the reflex response of always appearing accusatory and making every issue appear as a reprimand. To the manager who IS MANAGED, it is a way of gaining the skill to be direct and affirming his role as a manager.

Management assertiveness is a skill like any other. It needs to be practiced and developed. Remember what it was like when you made your first occupied bed. You were not sure that the patient would survive the experience. With constant practice it became second nature. You can develop the same degree of confidence and ability with these management assertiveness techniques *if you are willing to practice them.*

THE STAFF PERFORMANCE RECORD

1) Defining the Need

This leads to a major problem unique to the managers of the nursing department that is not an issue for managers of any other department. The nursing department in long term care is generally the only department that is in operation twenty-four hours a day, seven days a week. It is quite possible that nursing staff who rotate shifts will work with a number of different managers. The common question asked by managers of long term care is "How do I know this staff member was not just told the same thing by the last unit manager on duty?" It is quite possible that different managers could have spoken to the same staff member about the same issue in a short period of time and not know it. A chronic staff problem could be brewing and none of the managers may be aware of it until the opportunity to discuss it collectively. Unfortunately, those opportunities for conferencing on staff issues in the nursing department can be few and far between.

Imagine that we are together for our monthly nurse manager's meeting. One of the unit managers mentions that she just discovered a staff member (Mary) feeding Mrs. Jones and discussed the importance of encouraging resident independence. On hearing that, another manager notes up that she too told Mary the same thing last week. A third manager quickly interjects that she also told Mary about that same thing only two days ago. At the meeting, it is uncovered that twelve out of the sixteen unit managers present have spoken to Mary about resident independence over the past five weeks. The opportunity to resolve a potential chronic staff problem has been lost when no record is available to identify who said what to whom and when.

Take this one step further. How thorough can a yearly performance appraisal be if there is no ongoing monitoring of a staff member's performance? How can a nurse manager complete an accurate performance appraisal when she may encounter a staff member only sporadically each month?

The unit manager's limited contact with some staff can hamper her effectiveness in completing a performance appraisal. She may only be able to evaluate an employee's performance based on limited contact. In this instance, a yearly evaluation will usually only recall the extremes - things the person did very poorly or things that were done extremely well.

A below average staff member can have a fairly weak appraisal simply because the manager completing it is not aware of this person's accomplishments. She may not know that this staff member has established a very supportive relationship with three residents, doing extra things for them at every opportunity. This narrowness in the appraisal can result in staff having a negative perception of the appraisal process and some even fearing the results. An even more contentious issue may present itself - what if there is a personality conflict between the manager performing the appraisal and the staff member being evaluated?

Before a solution to these concerns is presented, allow me to throw in one more significant factor regarding performance evaluation. If staff are made accountable for their performance, what makes managers accountable for theirs? If the manager who IS MANAGED and those who MUST MANAGE are given no direction in areas where they need to improve, they will not change. In some organizations there exists a double standard. If a staff member is not performing his job well, he will hear about it. If a manager is not performing her job well, it may be glossed over or ignored. Managers within an organization require the same degree of performance expectation as staff. This means that standards of performance for unit managers must be clearly defined and monitored.

2) Providing the Solution

A solution to all of these issues is the Staff Performance Record. The purpose of this tool is to maintain an ongoing record of a staff member's performance throughout the year. It can be compiled in a card or file folder format and stored in the medicine cupboard under lock and key. This location assures confidentiality, with only the unit managers having access to it. Even though it is placed in a secured location, all staff have the freedom to read their own at any time.

When a manager corrects or praises a staff member's performance, what was discussed and the date is recorded on the file card and then initialed by the manager and the employee.

Let us turn back to the scenario about Mary inappropriately feeding a resident. After this is brought to Mary's attention by the manager on duty, it is recorded on Mary's Staff Performance Record. Three days later another manager speaks to Mary about a similar issue, that is also recorded. A week later another manager speaks to her again about the same thing. The third entry raises a red flag. It is now the third manager's responsibility to either speak to Mary about the reoccurrence of the issue or bring it to the attention of the director of resident care. The manager responsible to talk to Mary after the third entry can now set very specific guidelines to assist Mary to deal with this issue. A potential chronic problem is "nipped in the bud."

It is important to emphasize that the third entry does not necessarily initiate immediate disciplinary action. What is more productive is to set specific guidelines and goals for the staff member to correct the behavior or problem - whether that is further training, questioning the manager if not sure what needs to be done, referring to the care plan, etc.

This is a process of problem solving rather than crisis intervention. Crisis intervention occurs when a problem is allowed to go unnoticed, then there is a flurry of activity to attempt to resolve it well after the fact. This becomes very time consuming and ineffective way to deal with any issue.

Each organization needs to make this process specific. All managers must know when to raise the red flag (how many times has the same issue been noted), what action is taken, by whom and when. This will be discussed shortly under the area of the Manager's Manual.

3) Ensuring a Fair Assessment

There is a second component to the Staff Performance Record that must be stressed. This form is intended to record a person's accomplishments, as well as his weaknesses. When a staff member is praised for his actions, it must also be recorded on his file card. This creates a fair evaluation. If a person knows that both his strengths and weaknesses are identified, then he is less fearful of the performance record being one-sided and becoming a manager's weapon with the potential to be used against him at any time.

The benefits of the Staff Performance Record when completing the yearly performance appraisal are evident.

a) The performance appraisal is not based on what one unit manager has encountered, but is the accumulated evaluation of all unit manager's over the year.

b) The appraisal not only communicates what you would like to see changed but what you like about the staff member's performance.

c) Specific examples are given to identify the need for corrective action to be taken.

d) Demonstrating a recurrence of specific behaviors justifies the recommendations suggested.

e) Personality conflicts between the manager completing the appraisal and the staff member being appraised are less of a factor in the evaluation process.

This establishes a very positive and supportive atmosphere surrounding performance appraisals. It ensures an objective and thorough evaluation.

We need to stop here for a moment to identify the common critiques of this tool. The EFFECTIVE manager sees this as a positive process to ensure growth and excitement among her staff. Staff are a valuable resource that should be developed, not easily discarded. Likewise she trusts her staff. She believes that they desire to do the best possible job. She is not afraid to fire if it is necessary, but staff are given the benefit of the doubt. This manager's objective is to direct the individual to help that person improve performance. Although dismissal is an option, it is one that is taken after more positive avenues are exhausted. She will enthusiastically implement this tool or something similar to achieve the desired result. What is interesting is the response from the manager who MUST MANAGE and the manager who IS MANAGED about the Staff Performance Record and the process described.

That manager who MUST MANAGE will often negatively critique the process as too much work. He believes that if you have a problem employee, the solution is to simply get rid of him and the problem will go away. To this manager, firing an employee is seen as the immediate and best solution. That means that rather than working with the identified staff member, all efforts are invested "to get that individual." Unfortunately dismissal is counterproductive. Staff are *the most valuable resource* within a long term care facility. When a staff member has worked in the organization for an extended period of time, then the organization has made a substantial investment in that person. Throwing away that investment is a significant loss to the organization. Aggressive dismissal in the manner expected by the manager who MUST MANAGE has a significant negative impact. It colors staff morale and trust. The belief that staff can be so easily "let go," communicates to all staff (including the most positive) that they are of little value within the organization.

The manager who IS MANAGED on the other hand critiques the Staff Performance Record and the identified process in a somewhat different way. This manager believes that it will not work. This person fears conflict and will always attempt to avoid it. This tool requires ongoing communication with an employee about performance. The manager who IS MANAGED has "his head in the sand" and would rather "look the other way" than deal with anything directly.

No matter what the strategy or tool we discuss, there will always be those who express *concerns meant to paralyze*.

4) Looking at the Whole Picture

The following summarizes the benefits of the Staff Performance Record:

    a)   During the yearly performance appraisal, each manager can effectively identify a staff member's strengths and weaknesses regardless of the amount of contact that was involved. By utilizing the comments of all managers on the performance record, this manager can evaluate on the entire year's performance, not just isolated instances.

b) No matter what relationship exists between the manager and staff member, the comments written on the Staff Performance Record forces the yearly appraisal to be objective and accurate. There can be little opportunity for the manager completing the appraisal to merely use her inferences to identify how well or poorly a staff member is doing.

c) Management has the opportunity to provide each staff member direction to improve their performance throughout the year. As behaviors, attitudes or work problems are identified, they can be resolved, rather than waiting until the year end to discuss them during the performance appraisal process.

d) Most importantly, the performance record makes the manager accountable.

MANAGERS AND ACCOUNTABILITY

1) Holding Your "Boss" Accountable

What is your course of action if you are an EFFECTIVE MANAGER who repeatedly identifies problem employees and your "boss" is one who IS MANAGED and does little about it? Unless you can make a strong enough case, there is nothing compelling your boss to take any action.

When the Staff Performance Record is completed, the details presented about a specific staff member are hard to overlook. The potential problem looming when a number of managers have identified concerns places the ball squarely in the court of your "boss" to take action further than your role may allow.

If your "boss" still does nothing to resolve the problem, you are protected should something further develop. If you find yourself being questioned by family, the union or even an inquest (should it develop that far), you can demonstrate that you have taken the necessary steps, documented and recorded your actions. It is now the responsibility of your "boss" to answer why nothing was done.

2) Holding Other Managers Accountable

Another level of accountability can be initiated by the Staff Performance Record. As each staff record is scanned by the director of resident care, the input of the unit managers is revealing. What can be found is that certain manager's names are missing completely, and other managers are only recording the weaknesses of staff and never their strengths. What has been uncovered are the managers who ARE MANAGED and those who MUST MANAGE.

a) Manager who IS MANAGED

If given the freedom, this manager would rarely document anything on the Staff Performance Record. The director of resident care has the opportunity to effectively evaluate this manager's performance and provide specific directions to enhance her ability to successfully manage. Once the file cards are reviewed by the director of resident care, it will be obvious to her that the initials of the manager who IS MANAGED will be absent. The director of resident care can then approach this manager and state - "In my department I expect all of my managers to record on the Staff Performance Record. The reason for that is to provide staff with consistent management. What will happen if it is not done is that staff will not know what is expected and what is not." If the unit manager does not comply and is still found not to be recording on the staff performance records, the next approach is straightforward "Jane I have not seen your name on those forms once. I expect that in the next month, you will identify specific staff and speak to them about what they are doing well and what they are doing poorly and record your comments on their Performance Record." Of course the director of resident care would record her discussions on that manager's performance record, following up with a complete discussion of this issue and the manager's progress at her yearly performance appraisal session.

147

b) Manager who MUST MANAGE

The managers who MUST MANAGE will be found on many of the Staff Performance Records. Needless to say, most if not all of the comments recorded will identify things staff do poorly, but will seldom praise staff for what they do well. Once this is discovered by the director of care, she can then approach that manager and say - "In my department I expect all managers to record not only staff weaknesses, but also what they do well. The reason for that is if staff believe management only sees what is negative, then it will affect staff morale and trust. What will happen when managers are perceived in that way is morale will drop and along with it quality of care." If the direction given is not followed through by this manager and she does not indicate staff accomplishments on the performance record, the next response by the director of care is - "Dorothy I still cannot find your initials indicating that any staff are doing a good job. In the next month I want you to find staff who are performing their job well, tell them you appreciate it and record it on their performance records."

Unless managers are held accountable nothing will change. In each situation both the manager who IS MANAGED and the manager who MUST MANAGE are given specific guidelines on how to change their behavior and develop the needed skills to become an EFFECTIVE MANAGER.

c) A Caution

Initiating the Staff Performance Record without being aware of the organizational culture where it is placed can be detrimental to all concerned. In a facility where staff morale and trust is already low, such a program may only encounter suspicion and resistance.

The best way to sell a program such as this is on a three month trial basis for only one unit. In this way there is the opportunity to demonstrate to staff and managers within the facility that the Staff Performance Record can affect positive changes in the work environment, as well as enhance staff/management relations. By the way, facilities with an open and trusting work environment would probably have little difficulty implementing this program and are likely doing something similar already.

CASE STUDY AND THE MANAGER'S MANUAL

A frequent lament by many nurse managers is -

"I do not know what is expected of me as a manager."

When this perception is held within an organization, the chances of managers within that setting being effective is unlikely. This is not due to the managers' lack of ability or desire to manage well, but to the lack of guidelines on how to manage in that organization. In fact, managers who do not know their role in dealing with staff issues and organizational responsibilities would have difficulty answering the following question:

> Could I start as a new manager in your facility and immediately know what is expected of me in most situations?
>
> If the answer is no, then how long would it take me to learn your role so that I could perform it well?

If the answer to the first question is no, then that leaves only one way to learn how to manage in your organization - through trial and error. I have to wait until enough time passes to allow me to encounter enough management experiences in your organization before I know how to function effectively. Not only does that mean my ability is hampered for that period of time, it is also a hard and ineffective way of learning. Let me pursue this further.

On the evening and night shifts, as well as weekends, the unit managers are the only managers within the building. When specific direction is lacking, I am in the awkward and uncomfortable position of learning by experience. I have to wait for a problem to arise, determine what I believe is the best course of action from my own experience, background and training. I then must wait again for a response from upper management to know if what I did was acceptable. Probably the only time I will hear anything is when my action creates some problem or difficulty. Hearing only when I am not performing to the expected standards of the organization may impede my confidence. I start second guessing the effectiveness of my judgment when another situation is encountered. Over time I will hedge my bets. I will tend to take less action rather than the possible wrong action. Lack of direction for any new manager results in creating an ineffective manager.

If a newly employed manager does not know how to deal with problems until after they are over, then both management consistency and that manager's confidence are weakened. That will eventually create problems for upper management. When middle management becomes "gun shy," or reluctant to take action, then the organization is placed in the situation of crisis intervention rather than problem solving. The consequences of inaction or ineffective action by middle management will mean that problems are overlooked or dealt with poorly. Upper management is then in the situation of "putting out fires" - dealing with issues as they explode, rather than when they occur. This is a tremendous waste of time, energy and resources. Had the problem been dealt with properly the first time by the manager who encountered it, it would not escalate to that degree.

When direction is not given to managers on how to perform their role, then the risks associated with managing become too great. If a manager discovers that dealing with staff problems only results in considerable stress to justify one's actions, then the tendency for some is to avoid "managing." Therefore, some managers learn to become the manager who IS MANAGED, avoiding possible conflicts. Others learn to survive in their role by becoming managers who MUST MANAGE, taking total control of every situation.

The solution is simple - create a Manager's Manual. This is a virtual 'how to' for managers on dealing with organizational issues in that facility. It can be an alphabetical list of the step-by-step process of the manager's *standards of performance.*

The manager's manual is created by the management team. Recording on a flip chart, the unit managers and director of resident care list as many issues as possible that a unit manager could encounter. Then each issue (or in some cases groupings of issues) are broken down step-by-step and transposed alphabetically to a binder labeled The Manager's Manual.

Let us work through an example. The recorder writes at the top of the flip chart - "Staff arriving late for work." The management team then lists the steps to be taken should any manager encounter a staff member arriving late. That includes identifying

- what the unit manager is to do if it is encountered for the first time.
- what is to be done if it is encountered the second or third time.
- when the unit manager is to bring it to the attention of the director of resident care.

Once the steps are identified, it is then recorded in the Manager's Manual.

From that point on, no matter who the manager, new or veteran, full time or part time, the guidelines and expectations are outlined on what to do when a staff member is late for duty. In this way it is ensured that management is consistent in its expectations and treatment of staff regardless of the manager on duty. The Manager's Manual can become very extensive, outlining the expected course of action on any issue - "bitching," not following the policy/procedure manual or care plans, doing unnecessary care, resident abuse, etc.

Once this manual is developed, any new manager can refer to it when experiencing a problem and know exactly what is expected of him. Such a support can only increase a new manager's confidence in assuming his role as an EFFECTIVE MANAGER.

Secondly, the manager who is managed can use this manual as a "cookbook" on how to manage. It is a very formal and straightforward manner to learn what to do to become an EFFECTIVE MANAGER.

Thirdly, the manager who MUST MANAGE now has set expectations for his performance. Any delineation from the defined steps within the manual makes him accountable for his actions. By learning what other managers do, he has the opportunity of acquiring the skills of the EFFECTIVE MANAGER.

Both the Staff Performance Record and the Manager's Manual set criteria for managers to ensure consistency in the demands they place on their staff. In this way, it is not only the positive staff who are supported and the negative staff who are required to change their behavior and attitudes, but also the managers who are made accountable for their actions and given the direction to effectively complete their job.

THE MASK OF MANAGEMENT

Most nurses know that their actions, as well as their attitude, can be communicated verbally or non verbally to any patients under their care. Many patients are always trying to read something from our behavior or mannerisms that will tell them how they are doing. The same holds true for managers and their staff. Not all staff are open and assertive enough to ask what we think or feel about subjects pertaining to work. Instead they try to read from us clues that may give them that information.

Imagine that my relationship with my staff is very positive. My staff respect me as their manager. We have developed a very close and trusting bond. After a manager's meeting I return to the unit obviously upset and angry, stating "I am tired of trying to solve things around here. Every time I try to deal with a problem I don't get anywhere with it except to get myself into more trouble." How quickly will staff bring another problem to my attention? Their feelings for me may inhibit their expressing any further problems, just to protect me from encountering further frustrations.

Staff are often unable to understand our frustrations as managers. In one of my seminars, I use a group exercise that assists facilities to identify and solve existing problems. In this exercise I ask the direct line staff from the facility to role play their managers and identify the problems they believe their managers experience. In most cases, the staff will respond "We can't do that. We don't know what the managers do."

That is the key. Most nurse managers in long term care have probably been a direct line caregiver at one time or another. As a result, they can probably relate well to what their staff experience. In contrast, our staff have not been managers. Without that experience, they cannot easily relate to what we do or encounter.

Many staff can take our comments literally. When they do not understand our frustrations, they can easily personalize what they hear us say or see us do. When we express our trepidations to staff, that may communicate a sense of hopelessness. Their response can easily be - "If our managers cannot see a way to get us out from under our problems, then how can we resolve them?"

In the same light as our patients view us as nurses, our staff see us as managers. The mask of management represents the demeanor that a manager must present to her staff that is objective, confident and open.

This is not to suggest that we do not have "bad days." Demonstrating to staff that we are "as human as they are" is important. As we demonstrate that we are able to accept certain limitations of staff under specific circumstances and situations, we need our staff to accept ours as well. To say to staff, "Let me have half an hour before we talk about any further problems. I have had a busy day and need to clear my head" is to demonstrate to staff that we have the same needs as they.

Staff have difficulty understanding managers who complain, or even worse, manager's who "bitch," gossiping about staff, managerial or organizational problems, complaints about stumbling blocks within the organization, about other managers, etc. Such negative, self-centered comments or actions only hamstring our staffs' ability to deal with their jobs effectively.

A further proponent of this mask of management is to establish a philosophy among the management team - we *agree to disagree* but we *agree to agree*. When something is brought to a management meeting, it is an expressed and practiced belief that any manager can freely express his opinion about what is being discussed, whether positive or negative - we agree to the right to disagree. On the other hand, once the management team decides on a course of action, then all managers must follow it - we agree to agree. That sets an expectation that all managers will work as a cohesive group to meet the defined objectives. If some managers leave the meeting believing - "this isn't going to work," then it won't. We have identified over and over again our ability to influence our staff in many ways. Our attitude can color the outcome of any project.

To agree to agree defines a specific philosophy for the management team. It dictates that all managers are expected to approach any decision as though they believed 100% in its success. It is at the next meeting when the decision can be accurately assessed and its continuation discussed - we can again agree to disagree.

There is a further component concerning the mask of management.

It is the ability to get "dirty." It is amazing when one watches a manager walk past something that has fallen on the floor, just to get a housekeeper to pick it up. Or a manager spends the time to find a nurse's aid because a resident needs a Kleenex. If we cannot do what the staff do, then we are telling our staff that what they do is beneath us and not important. "Getting dirty" is the expectation that managers will work shoulder to shoulder with their staff. This not only enhances rapport in management/staff relations, but it is also the best "on the job training." We then have the ability to teach by example.

Lastly, the mask of management encompasses one other side. Staff need to see that managers encourage the freedom to have fun in the work place. Encouraging staff to have fun in their job is not only an opportunity for them to release the ongoing emotional tension that can be created in this line of work, but it also adds a needed dimension in the quality of life for our residents. Fun is part of the job of all members of the facility. Yet it never ceases to amaze me when I see a manager tell her staff to be involved in resident recreational activities, but she does not take her own advice. During a sing along on the unit, the staff are pushed to be involved and the manager is seen leaning silently against the door. An EFFECTIVE MANAGER is one who is able to relate to her staff at all levels, not just as the "boss."

As a manager, I know what is expected of me.
I am backed in what I say and supported in what I do.

SUMMARY

We complain bitterly about ineffective staff and their impact on the residents, the unit and the organization. Unfortunately, there is nothing more dangerous than an ineffective manager. It is the manager who sets the overall tone of the unit or department. One ineffective manager can incapacitate an entire team of competent staff, thereby creating a devastating effect on the quality of life of the residents living on that unit.

As we have established, it is not solely the manager's skills that preclude her success. It is also the environment where that manager works. Maintaining our original assertion that the level of care the staff gives to the resident is totally reflected by how well the facility takes care of its staff, clearly dictates a need for well defined and consistent staff supports within the facility. It is now time to examine the supports required by both staff and managers.

Chapter Seven

DEALING WITH TODAY'S ISSUES

There are two ways of coping with organizational problems - through problem solving or crisis intervention. Effective organizational problem solving is an active process. It involves identifying and dealing with issues as they arise. There are four components that contribute to effective problem solving:

OWNERSHIP - expectation of a responsibility to take action.

COMMUNICATION - a means of getting information to others.

ANALYSIS - an objective way of investigating an issue to determine possible solutions.

RESOLUTION - the freedom and ability to deal with it.

Crisis intervention on the other hand is reactive. When ownership and communication do not exist, the manager is left to wait until a problem becomes highly visible before it can be addressed - a process of "putting out fires."

It is possible to understand crisis intervention by comparing it with fire fighting.

In fire fighting, a forest ranger sits in his tower waiting until he sees smoke and flames before he can spring into action.

In crisis intervention a problem is allowed to lie dormant, festering until it ignites into a major issue that forces the attention of management.

When a fire ignites, fire fighters must give everything they have to prevent the fire from getting away from them.

Solving a crisis requires the organization and its managers to invest all available resources and energies to extinguish it.

Once the fire is extinguished, the job is not over. The remnants of the fire must be cleared and things that were burned must be restored.

Fires leave scars. The blackened area will be visible for a long time until it heals over.

Fire fighting can be a stressful job. Extinguishing fires as they ignite becomes a never ending battle. One fire is quenched, only to have another flare up elsewhere. There is no time to look ahead to prevent the next - a fire fighter must deal with each fire as it arises. He is guaranteed that there will always be a fire igniting, requiring the pattern to begin again.

The after-effects of crisis intervention leads to a further round of clean-up, as well as re-construction, with little time for progress before the next problem erupts.

Similarly, when an organization is in constant crisis intervention, it will not be easy to recover from the damage it has caused to staff morale and trust.

Crisis management can be very stressful. As soon as one crisis is resolved, another appears. Moving from crisis to crisis leaves no time to look ahead to prevent the next - a never ending cycle. This pattern eventually exhausts all managers, disintegrating their effectiveness, efficiency and excitement.

The slogan "Only you can prevent forest fires," is also applicable to managers and crisis intervention - "*Only you can prevent crisis management.*"

One way to identify whether an organization employs problem solving or crisis intervention is to determine the degree that staff need their managers to be able to function. The more independent the staff, the more efficient the organization. When appropriate problem solving mechanisms are in place, staff are able to deal well with everyday problems on their own. This participatory process creates a level of independence that allows management to invest their energies in planning for tomorrow. This ends the need to constantly look back at yesterday to find what is unresolved and soon to raise its dreaded head.

As there are pyromaniacs when it comes to real fires, our organizations also have their fire starters - the negative staff. The characteristics of negative staff to constantly harp on weaknesses within the organization, blowing them out of proportion for their own gain is akin to starting fires. Their needling and "bitching" continually stirs the ashes of discontent and mistrust. They are always probing for the vulnerable areas where kindling is dry and easy to ignite. When there is nothing visible within the organization to counter their accusations, they will eventually contaminate all that is happening. When that occurs, the evaluation by staff that "they (management) don't care" can easily be read into every action, every infraction, everything.

On the other hand, a supportive, open organization stands behind its staff and counters the forces of the negative. It continually demonstrates to its team members that they are important and respected. It is an organization that gets its staff excited.

THE UNION

Ineffective managers will often proclaim - "Unions are the problem." These managers are reluctant to involve staff in the problem solving process believing that little can be accomplished when a union is present. If that were the case then why are effective managers with unionized staff still able to have active, coordinated teams? Is it the unions who are unreasonable and do not listen or the managers who are unreasonable and do not listen, or both? The age old question - "What came first, the chicken or the egg?"

If a manager is not willingly to listen to me and deal with the issues I am experiencing, then there is a need to get his attention. When an organization has the history of only dealing with crisis, then to get a problem solved leaves no choice but to make it into a crisis. Unfortunately, that is how some unions are used - creating one crisis after another to direct management to solve the staff's problems.

By the way, in defense of managers, some unions and union members only know one way to solve problems and that is through crisis creation. Everything we have just discussed about managers and organizations can be said about some unions in their process of solving problems and their perception of management. They can believe and promote a philosophy among their members that professes that there is only one course of action "against them" (management) - confrontation on every situation no matter what the management professes their philosophy to be.

Unfortunately, the block to effective problem solving with a union may not be local. An effective manager may demonstrate to his staff and local union representatives that the organization is supportive of its staff and encourages a team effort, only to find that the national union body preaches that managers cannot be trusted. They constantly attempt to instill in all of its members a selfish philosophy - "We want what we want when we want it" regardless of the logistic or financial constraints that exist. What came first the chicken or the egg?

Regardless of the answer, the ineffective manager uses the union as further justification to bar staff from active participation within the organization. That in turn reinforces to the union that their philosophy is right and the cycle continues.

The effective manager on the other hand will see those dynamics as only a further challenge. This manager will always conflict with the union's perception. She will create a team atmosphere by encouraging her staff to take ownership for the problems that exist and ensuring that they are listened to. No matter the outside forces that exist, her staff will be excited about what they do and where they do it.

AVOIDING A CRISIS

A riddle for you - *If ten staff are working ineffectively because of an inappropriate care system, what happens when you add one more staff member? You will get eleven staff working ineffectively.*

The demand for more staff is a universal one. In many instances it is probably very realistic given our increasingly complex clientele. However, it is often inaccurate. In an organization that employs a crisis intervention focus, the first cry to deal with organizational problems and inadequacies is to demand more staff. When poor team dynamics and involvement exists, the staff just added are quickly sucked into the organizational quagmire and do little to resolve the problems that exist.

In actual fact, when an organization is problem solving oriented, the actual staffing needs can be accurately defined. The organization is then evaluating the increased demands of its resident population, not attempting to compensate for any organizational inadequacies. In fact when staffing is added, it creates an immediate and dramatic improvement on efficiency and effectiveness.

LACK OF OWNERSHIP AND CRISIS MANAGEMENT

Let us create a fictitious one hundred and fifty bed facility, consisting of three separate units - unit A, B, and C. Staff work on all units, rotate all shifts and are randomly assigned resident groupings. The units are losing resident clothing.

When staff are haphazardly assigned to units and residents, they will often have limited knowledge of the idiosyncrasies of each client and limited ownership of the unit where they work. Let me demonstrate with a simple example of a resident who has fourteen underwear in her dresser drawer.

The staff member assigned to this lady the first two days of the week discovers that she has nine underwear. Not knowing the resident, it is likely that this staff member will not question the location of the other five underwear. Another staff member is assigned to this resident the next two days and discovers that she has five underwear in her dresser drawer. Again without knowledge of the existence of the other underwear, their location will not be questioned. As staff rotate each shift and each unit, the only time the missing underwear may be questioned is when there are none available. Staff now are required to waste considerable time looking for underwear. Remember the mosquito annoyances - what bothers staff the most are simple little things that they encounter again and again.

The end result is obvious. Family will then be approached to buy mother more underwear. The family's response "Where are the fourteen underwear she had in her drawer just last week?" Laundry and housekeeping are brought into the equation. If they are also isolated into their departments and do not take ownership of a specific unit or portion of the resident population, then their response will be the famous lament - "I don't know." Invariably, family will become upset and approach the manager in charge of the unit. If that manager does not have the means that allow her to analyze and resolve the problem, or the authority to make a decision, little can be done. The family will be forced to bring the loss of their mother's underwear to the attention of the upper management. Now upper management is dealing with an issue that should be resolved at the unit level, and the organization is required to invest its time and resources to solve what was at one time a simple problem.

Of course the resolution process is dependent on the type of manager involved. The manager who IS MANAGED will do little or nothing until the problem grows to where it can no longer be hidden. Once resident and family complaints reach the point where he can no longer ignore them, he will act. We know this type of manager is not comfortable or adept enough to involve the team to solve the problem at hand, so he will unilaterally change the policy on handling personal linen. His lack of knowledge of the idiosyncrasies of the unit, staff needs and resident profiles will invariably create a policy that is not workable, only intensifying the situation.

The manager who MUST MANAGE doesn't trust others to have the ability to solve their own problems. He automatically changes the policy on his own as well. His misperception of the needs of his organization will also result in a policy being implemented that is not easily workable.

In each of these cases, the personal linen policy has been changed without input by either nursing or laundry staff who handle resident clothing. The possibility that this unilateral solution will resolve the problem will be remote. The fire starter, the negative staff, now have an opening. They will zero in on how the problem was resolved stating "No one asks us what is needed around here." Even worse, the solution created may result in more problems than the original one.

Effective problem solving requires ownership - expectation of responsibility to take action. Without ownership, there is no communication - a means of getting information to others. Without communication there can be no analysis - an objective way of investigating an issue to determine possible solutions. Without analysis, there can be no resolution - freedom and ability to deal with it. What exists is a crisis. The overall impact is a loss in efficiency and effectiveness which will impede the level of quality care, decaying the excitement of those doing that care and decreasing the quality of life for the residents involved.

The solution is to instill ownership. This can only be done with the creation of a team atmosphere through a concept called The Client Centered Approach.

OVERVIEW: THE CLIENT CENTERED APPROACH

The Client Centered Approach (similar to Primary or Modular Care), allows a facility to:

⇒ achieve the goals of quality of life for the residents
⇒ establish staff and team efficiency and effectiveness
⇒ coordinate interdepartmental involvement
⇒ minimize bureaucracy

The impact of such an approach is to create effective organizational problem solving.

In many organizations staff assignments are randomly made, with minimal consistent contact of any one staff to a unit, let alone any one resident. This lack of ownership places limitations on the freedom of direct line staff to adjust and define the care routine. Communication between shifts and other departments can be minimal and general. When an organization is divided into departments, not teams, problems and information must take a long and complicated path from the nursing staff to the unit manager, to the director of resident care, to other department heads, to their staff, and back before being resolved.

A fifty bed unit in a hundred and fifty bed facility is the size of many small nursing homes or hospitals. The three units involved cannot be totally run as one given that neither is similar to the other. Each differs in their resident make-up, levels of care and functioning, and in the number of staff on each shift. This means that each has slightly different needs, requiring some flexibility in implementing organizational policies and procedures. To be effective, such a facility must provide each unit with a degree of autonomy. This freedom to be self-governed allows each unit to adapt the overall organizational mandates to the specific individuality of each its setting.

The Client Centered Approach places the responsibility for resident care and problem solving at the team level. It flattens the organization and divides a large facility into distinct modular units. Each unit operates with autonomy, having its own full and part time staff. The unit's staff does not just encompass the nursing department, but every other department that may have contact with the resident - recreation, social services, housekeeping, dietary, etc.

This concept encompasses the full dynamics of team involvement. Consistent staffing at all levels not only enhances communication and problem solving, but ensures that everyone is aware of specific issues of individual residents, improving the quality of care provided. In essence, these units are self-contained, almost as small facilities within a large facility. They have control over budgetary expenditures, equipment, supplies, even personalizing the home's philosophy of care to fit the specific needs of the resident population living on that unit.

OBJECTIVES OF THE CLIENT CENTERED APPROACH

The objectives of the Client Centered Approach are as follows:

- to decrease the number of different staff working with individual residents each day, seven days per week period.
- to provide each resident with a client advocate on each shift.
- to maximize individualized/personalized resident care.
- to ensure consistency in care and programming.
- to provide a consistent link between the resident and all departments.
- to enhance team functioning and organizational problem solving.

163

COMMON CLIENT CENTERED APPROACH TERMINOLOGY

Staffing Pairs   - a full time staff member and that person's regular part time replacement.

Advocate Team   - the six staff (three full time and their three part time replacements) who are assigned to one resident group.

Resident Grouping   - the number of residents assigned to the advocate team is determined by dividing the number of full time equivalents on duty during the day shift into the number of residents on the unit.

Care Team   - all members of a unit, encompassing all departments - RN, RNA, nurse's aide, recreation, housekeeping, dietary, maintenance, etc.

TEAM CONFIGURATION AND STAFF ASSIGNMENT

An organization that randomly assigns direct line staff to resident care each shift, creates the possibility of twenty one different caregivers being assigned to one resident over a seven day period (a different staff member each shift, each day). This inconsistent assignment of direct line staff to residents has been demonstrated to have the following effects:

- an increase in resident aggressive or withdrawn behavior
- an increase in custodial care
- a loss of resident individuality
- a lack of consistency in care
- a creation of "islands" among departments and shifts
- wasted time and resources
- increased pressure on those who are conscientious about their work

When the Client Centered Approach is implemented, those problems can be overcome. With this model there is the ability to reduce the number of different staff caring for any one resident to as few as six in a seven day period. Successful implementation of this model focuses on the staff's master rotation schedule.

A true master schedule does not only identify the consistent scheduling of full time staff, but also identifies:

1) A consistent scheduling for part time staff.
2) The advocate team this staff member belongs to.
3) The unit this person is on.
4) The group of residents the staff are assigned.

1) Part Time Schedule

We must first discuss the part time schedule. During each rotation (the number of weeks required to repeat the same schedule pattern), the master schedule always has the same number of replacement shifts that must be filled (excluding sick time and vacations). Consistent part time assignments can be accomplished by simply taking the number of replacement shifts and evenly dividing them by the number of part time staff available. Each part time person is then assigned the replacement shifts of one full time staff member throughout the rotation. In this way the master schedule creates paired groupings of staff - a full time staff member and that person's consistent part time replacement. It is important that these staffing pairs be matched into advocate teams.

2) The Advocate Team

The advocate team consists of six staff - three full time and their consistent part time replacements. All six are assigned to the same group of residents. To create a balanced advocate team without assignment conflicts, it is important that a full time staff member working the day shift is matched with another full time staff member who is simultaneously working the evening shift, and another who is simultaneously working the night shift. In this way, when the Client Advocate (part or full time) is on the day shift, there will always be one on the evening and night shift. This results in one of the six Client Advocates on duty on each shift, every day of the week.

3) Resident Groupings

To create resident groupings, the resident population of a unit is simply divided by the number of full time staff equivalents on duty during the day shift. To demonstrate this, imagine that a unit consisted of thirty five residents with five staff on duty during the day shift (the staff/resident ratio varies dramatically from facility to facility). There would then be five groups of seven residents each called resident groupings.

It is imperative that these groupings not be randomly chosen. The groupings must be arranged by the team based on the care requirements of individual residents. Each advocate should represent a mixture of heavy to lighter care, balancing the work load and the room location of each resident to prevent undue running. If a consistent complaint is made by a number of staff of one group, then that is an indication that the groups are unbalanced and there needs to be some adjusting to make them even.

Implementing the Client Centered Approach on a unit with thirty five residents and five full time staff equivalents on the day shift would create five advocate teams, each comprised of six staff (three full time and three part time) and seven residents to each staff assignment.

It is important to stress with direct line staff that being assigned to a group of residents does not mean that they are solely responsible for the care of those residents. Care is still completed as a team, sharing responsibility for baths, beds, etc. Should the Client Advocate be off the unit for lunch or coffee and his/her resident requests to go to the bathroom or to be served her lunch, the fact that the resident's Client Advocate is not present does not absolve other staff of those duties. Care is the responsibility of the entire team on the unit. The role of the Client Advocate goes beyond just the physical care and standard responsibilities.

ROLE OF THE CLIENT ADVOCATE

For many, advocacy is considered a passive role - the process of waiting for someone to be wronged before action is taken. In the Client

Centered Model, the client advocate has an active role - promoting resident individuality and ensuring a positive experience.

The Client Advocate assumes a role similar to that of a family member or significant other who is caring for an older person. In caring for an older client in the community, any professional (physician, physiotherapist, counselor, community health nurse, etc.) would rely heavily on the family caregiver as:

⇒ *a source of information.*

⇒ *a focal point in providing instructions so that they can be clarified for the older client at a later date.*

⇒ *someone who will ensure that things are followed through.*

⇒ *someone who will observe and report the results of any treatment or programs initiated.*

Likewise, the Client Advocate provides the same resource and supports.

The Client Advocate becomes the contact person to define need, relate history, give instructions, follow-through on interventions, evaluate effectiveness, and detail problems. In essence, the Client Advocate becomes the resource to other professionals who have less contact with a specific resident, but who need detailed information in order to function effectively. Having a consistent Client Advocate on each shift ensures that this assistance and information is always available.

The client advocate responsibilities are as follows:

1) **Individualized Care**

This not only involves the day-to-day care issues but goes much further. The Client Advocate is responsible to uncover and communicate issues pertaining to the resident's personal history; emotional, psychological, physical, environmental, spiritual and social needs; current and past problems that may impact on the resident's present situation; physical, social and mental abilities; and personal idiosyncrasies that must be met to provide personalized/individualized care.

2) **Assessment**

The Client Advocate is a major contributor in the completion of any assessment - functional, recreation/social, psychological, medication, activities of daily living, etc.

3) **Advocate**

One of the most significant functions of the Client Advocate is acting as an advocate for specific residents. The Client Advocate supports, represents or speaks on behalf of the resident regarding any decisions concerning routines, living arrangements or needs, care conferences, moves, treatments, etc.

4) **Evaluation**

The Client Advocate is utilized as a major resource in evaluating the effectiveness of programming and care strategies implemented by the care team, as well as the overall response of the resident to living within the facility.

Diagrammatically, the Client Advocate's relationship to the resident and other departments can be represented as follows:

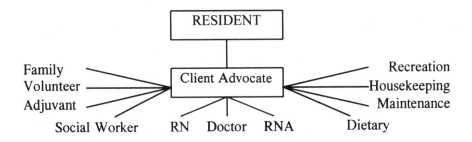

An immediate response by some professionals when looking at this diagram is that too much "authority" is given to nursing staff. In actual fact the Client Advocate does not have authority, but becomes a resource person for other staff. If the doctor has placed a resident on a certain medication, it is logical that during his rounds, he would want to talk to the Client Advocate on duty to see if there has been any change in the resident's behavior or functioning. Likewise, if maintenance is planning to change the faucets in a resident's washroom, it would make sense to inform the Client Advocate. If the resident cannot tolerate the added stimuli, it may be more practical to do the work at a time when the resident is not in the room, rather than to upset her. Should the recreation staff want to know the best time for a resident's activity, the Client Advocate becomes the most logical resource.

Imagine the support to volunteers and family that the Client Centered Approach provides. Volunteers are not only assigned specific residents, but also linked with that resident's Client Advocate. This guarantees that there will always be someone there to support them while on the unit. Similarly, family will see the same staff members involved with their parent, providing significant support and contact for information.

An additional benefit of the Client Centered Approach involves evaluation and accountability. When direction or intervention is discussed at a care conference, there is now a specific and limited number of staff required to follow through. For example, if it is decided that a resident is capable of learning to feed herself with a spoon using her right hand, then the Client Advocates involved with that resident are required to implement the intervention. It is obvious that the rapport of the Client Advocate with that resident would be a significant asset in motivating her to attempt this degree of independence.

Secondly, there are now only six staff (the advocate team) involved in giving instructions on what has to be done. This ensures more consistency in what is asked of the resident by staff who have learned how to communicate with her and are sensitive to her physical and psychological limits. In this way demands placed on the resident are more realistic.

Under the Client Centered Approach, problems encountered or changes in the resident's ability need not wait until the next care conference. The Client Advocates can immediately discuss the response of the resident with the registered staff or physiotherapist in order to adapt what is being asked. Even if the Client Advocate should be off the unit during certain meal times, she is responsible to have another staff member assist the resident to learn to use a spoon. Now the possibility for success of any program or intervention has greatly improved.

Under the Client Centered Approach, evaluation of what has been requested is more thorough and accurate. When registered staff are charting the resident's progression, they need only talk with the Client Advocate on duty. At a care conference when the care plan is reviewed, the Client Advocate will be able to comment on how well the resident has responded.

Furthermore, the Client Centered Approach ensures accountability of resident care. When things are not followed through or completed properly, then specific staff can be identified and approached in order to clarify their role or determine problems in performing what is required. Under this model, staff become very aware that they are expected to take ownership for their actions and all realize that how they perform their job has a tremendous impact on the quality of care provided. Now individual staff who have difficulty with certain duties can be easily identified so that they can be assisted in improving their performance.

POTENTIAL CHALLENGES

When a hoyer lift is introduced to a unit, staff are given a specific set of instructions on how to use it. It doesn't matter where that lift is used, in what facility, which unit, or who is using it, the instructions are universal. That is not the case with the Client Centered Approach. Even though guidelines for implementation can be provided, each unit will need to fine tune the concept to adapt it to the idiosyncrasies specific to that unit. Many of these issues will not surface until the model is introduced. It must be stressed to all staff and managers that "problems" are the only way to know how to adapt the concept. Then and only then can steps be taken by the team to decide what needs to be done. The following are some common issues encountered in the implementation of the Client Centered Approach.

a) Off Shifts

Off shifts are the evening and night shift. These usually change the configuration of the resident assignment. A unit that has a different number of staff on duty with each shift - i.e. five staff on the day shift, four on evenings and two on nights - will have to adjust the assignments for the off shifts.

On the day shift, a thirty five bed unit will have a staff/resident assignment of seven residents (the basic number for each advocate team), but on the evening shift when four staff are on duty, three staff will be assigned to nine residents and one will be assigned to eight residents. This is not as complicated as it appears. The number of staff on each unit is consistent each week, therefore once the assignments are made, they also become consistent.

The resident assignment on evening shift is not randomly chosen. It is based on the advocate team. The assignment would appear as follows:

⇒ The four staff on afternoons must each be assigned their normal grouping.
⇒ The fifth group of seven residents is then divided among the four staff.

Once this resident grouping is created, it need not be changed. With a master schedule, once a pattern is identified it is repeated in every rotation. In an eight week rotation, this staffing pattern occurs every six weeks. When it is repeated, those are assigned the same additional residents. In this way, staff would know their assignment well in advance and have an opportunity to familiarize themselves with those residents before moving onto the evening shift, ensuring consistency in care and programming.

The night shift is not as crucial and can easily be divided. If there are only two staff on duty and thirty five residents on the unit, each staff member would be assigned their normal resident grouping and consistently divide the remaining residents.

b) Sick Time and Staff Vacation
In the event of sick time and staff vacation, the most appropriate replacement strategy is to have a part time member of that advocate team replace the person who is off. In this way the advocate team stays intact. In a unionized facility where staff replacement is based on seniority, some complaints may arise. This can be overcome by negotiating that for the first nine months of the year, part time staff

within a advocate team would replace staff who are off sick or on vacation. If by the ninth month, there are discrepancies where lower seniority part time staff have more accumulated hours than those of higher seniority, then those of higher seniority are called to replace any staff for the last three months until the imbalance is rectified.

Replacement for long term disability is the easiest to accommodate. Those shifts can be assigned to any staff, as long as it is the same part time or group of part time each week for the duration of the person's illness. Consistency in staffing is therefore maintained.

It is consistency in staff replacement that is the priority in the Client Centered Approach. Given the realities of a 24 hour operation, staff must be aware that the master schedule cannot guarantee 100% consistency no matter what efforts are employed. There will always be a time when a staff member who is not part of a specific advocate team or even a regular member on a unit will be assigned a group of residents she does not know. Under the Client Centered Approach, the impact of that occurrence on care and team functioning will be minimal. Random assigning of staff becomes the exception rather than the rule. At least with the degree of consistency that can be maintained, there are enough regular members on the unit during that shift to provide the "new" staff member the necessary direction and support, ensuring that the routines and approaches are maintained.

c) Double Booking

With any master schedule there will be times when members of the six person advocate team (those assigned to the same group of residents) may be working the same shift for one or two days every rotation (possibly when one staff has moved to the day shift and the other is about to switch to the evening shift). Even though this is a break in the scheduling pattern, it will be a consistent occurrence, repeating itself every five weeks (the length of the master schedule rotation). That staff member would then be assigned to the free group of seven residents. Even though not ideal, that staff member will know which residents will be under her care during that period, this person now becomes a member of a second advocate team. Knowing that, allows this staff member the opportunity to prepare for the resident care to be given. Again it is the consistency that is important. Staff have advanced warning about who they will be caring for and know that specific assignment will be repeated in every rotation of the master schedule.

d) Utilizing Four Hour or Spot Shifts

Many units regularly schedule four hour shifts. Other facilities on certain shifts will have an extra staff member on duty (spot shifts), either to accommodate scheduling changes, or specific activities regularly arranged on that unit for that day of the week. The four hour and spot shift staff do not become direct members of the advocate team. Instead, their role is to assist the Client Advocates. They would be assigned specific tasks - i.e. bathing certain residents. Their duties will vary depending on the needs of the team or certain residents.

For example, a staff member working the four hour shift may be asked to bath a resident the same day each week for three weeks. On the fourth week, that person may be required to bath a different resident in that time slot. The rationale for this change is dependent on the resident or advocate team. During the first three weeks this resident's bath was straightforward and could be completed by anyone with only minimal direction provided by the Client Advocate. If during the fourth week it was decided at the care conference that this resident could be taught to assist in her bath, then the Client Advocate would want to be involved in that task rather than the four hour staff person. This again would ensure consistency in approach and effective evaluation of the success of this intervention.

e) Length of Advocate Team Assignment

The length of time staff are assigned to one group of residents can vary from one to three months and depend on a number of factors. That decision is left to the discretion of the care team.

It is best when first initiating the Client Centered Approach to begin at the low end. Initially many staff may be unsure of what is expected of them. Even though the concept may be understood, its implementation and effect is not yet known. Much of the "old" way of thinking about resident care may result in some staff seeing this as "more work." They may resist the concept of the Client Centered Approach only because they believe that the length of time assigned to a resident group and the associated work load is unfair.

It is best to begin with a one month trial period. After that month the assignments can be reviewed and the decision made on what is an appropriate duration. If after that month there are a number of complaints about the work load by staff assigned a specific resident group, then it is not the time factor that is the issue, but the imbalance in the group arrangements. In that instance, the groups need to be re-adjusted until having one group of residents really doesn't matter. When staff begin to realize that the groupings are all about the same in the amount of time required, the number who need to be lifted, the number who are difficult and so on, the length of time assigned to a group becomes irrelevant.

Suggested Steps in Implementing The Client Centered Approach

1. Establish consistent part time scheduling.
2. Assign the same part time to the same full time each week.
3. Create the advocate teams by matching staffing pairs who work opposite shifts (when one is on the day shift, the other is on the evening and the other on the night shift).
4. Create resident groupings by dividing the number of residents on the unit by the number of full time staff equivalents on the day shift, arranging the groupings by resident care and location on the unit.
5. Assign advocate teams to specific resident groupings.
6. Consistently assign staff of other departments to the unit (housekeeping, recreation, dietary, etc.).

SUMMARY

An organization is a conglomerate of people attempting to achieve a common goal. Unless that goal is defined by all segments of that group, then there can be no coordinated effort to achieve it. The days of the autocrat, the omnipotent manager, are long gone.

It is necessary for any organization to progress forward rather than being constantly shackled by past issues. If you attempt to move ahead without your staff knowing where you are going, you will lose them along the way.

Chapter Eight

CREATING THE UPWARD SPIRAL

We have all heard of the Downward Spiral - the deterioration of an organization's ability to perform its job effectively. The Upward Spiral is:

The process of enhancing an organization's ability to do its job even more effectively.

One key component to achieve this upward acceleration is effective communication. In our understanding of relationships at the beginning of the text, communication was demonstrated as one of the foundations from which a strong and positive relationship can be built.

In a relationship, the more the partners talk with each other the more they understand each other's perceptions, needs, aspirations, fears, and values. This insight into the other's world ensures understanding. The more we discuss, the more we uncover and raise issues before they become serious concerns. This means that we will generally deal with each concern at the appropriate time, utilizing each other's abilities to resolve things as they arise.

When staff and managers see themselves as partners, they set very specific expectations of what is needed to fulfill that role. They consciously build thorough and ongoing communication strategies to allow them to work effectively together. This communication pattern establishes a solid foundation to the relationship. It provides an opportunity for each to discover what the other team members value and how they perceive any given situation.

In the four parts to effective problem solving - ownership, communication, analysis and resolution - the Client Centered Approach establishes the needed ownership. Effective communication on the other hand involves a loop.

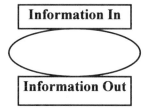

This process of getting information to and from others can successfully lead to the elimination of "islands" discussed earlier - management versus staff, shift versus shift, and department versus department. The challenge in a twenty-four hour, seven day a week operation is to ensure that the communication loop stays intact. Certain strategies can accomplish this well. They include: the Unit Meeting, the Facility Meeting, the Newsletter, the Suggestion Box and Upper Management contact.

THE UNIT MEETING

1) Defining The Need

The more autonomy provided any unit, the more effective the staff will be in problem solving. The unit meeting enhances that autonomy. It ensures effective communication between staff and managers, and provides a vehicle to resolve a problem before it can become a crisis. This meeting is regularly scheduled and involves the direct line caregivers normally assigned to that unit (including the unit manager, nursing, housekeeping, dietary and recreation staff). The goal of the unit meeting is to discuss the organizational issues affecting staff in performing their job.

The first response by some managers and staff is "We don't have time for this." In any organization, time is a constant. No matter what is involved, the investment of time becomes an option of choice. If a problem exists that hampers staffs efficiency to complete their job, then time is being wasted by constantly trying to compensate for that problem. The other alternative is to invest the time to solve the problem. In either option, the choice is to consciously solve the problem or waste time living with the problem. It is obvious that it is more prudent to invest the time to resolve the problem than deal with it day in and day out until it becomes a crisis.

2) Setting A Schedule and An Agenda

The scheduling of this meeting must be consistent - e.g. 1430 hours, every second Tuesday. Unless it is structured in this way, staff and the unit will not have the opportunity to adjust their routines to accommodate the meeting. Being scheduled in this manner has the potential of creating some conflict. Not all staff who work on that unit will be working at the time of the meeting.

This can spur a legitimate complaint by those working evening and night shifts that they are not represented at the meeting. The misconception that the meeting only benefits those staff working the day shift can be easily construed. You can hear the lament by the negative staff already "They don't ask us on afternoons (nights, weekends, whenever) what we think."

The solution is to set an agenda with a slight difference - identify a contact person next to every item on the agenda. This contact person is a direct line staff member scheduled to work on the day of the meeting. This person's role is to allow staff unable to attend the meeting to pass on their concerns or suggestions, and to receive feedback after the meeting. This secures the communication loop - information in/ information out.

A contact person does away with the need for notes. Few are adept enough in their writing skills to communicate through a piece of paper exactly what they want. By having the opportunity to talk to a contact person before the meeting, a staff member can say "Mary you are discussing personal linen at the next meeting. Make sure you add this about the afternoon shift . . ." The contact person may impose her bias in what is presented, but at least the information will be more detailed than what any staff member could write in a note. The first part of the communication loop has been achieved - information in.

Once the minutes have been released, they may not be clear to those who did not attend the meeting. The role of the contact person after the meeting is to answer any questions regarding what was discussed. Of course the contact person identified in the minutes must be the same contact person on the agenda.

Prior to the meeting Mary was approached to have the concerns of the afternoon staff discussed. Afternoon staff see nothing in the minutes about that issue. Staff can now approach Mary and ask "Mary, why didn't you present the points concerning the afternoon shift?" Mary's response may be "I presented them, but we ran out of time and had to place them on the agenda for the next meeting." After a meeting, staff now have the opportunity to clarify what was said and why. Information out - the loop is complete.

The contact person should not be the unit manager for the following reasons:

a) *The unit manager at the change of shift is usually giving report.* That requires the staff working the evening shift to arrive earlier than normal or the staff on the night shift to stay later in order to talk with that unit manager. Assigning a direct line staff member as the contact person eliminates that awkwardness. In a two week period, direct line staff assigned as the contact person would probably have brief encounters at the change of shift with almost all staff who work that unit. As one is coming on duty and the other is going off, they can share what they want discussed at the meeting.

b) *The unit meeting is the staff's problem solving mechanism.* Having the manager as the contact person can create a perception that some staff have more power than others. Discussing the issue in advance with the unit manager can be interpreted as an unfair advantage that precludes the need for any further discussion. You can just hear the negative staff when the manager shares that Jane has talked to her about what is on the agenda - "That cinches that. Whatever Jane wants, the boss does. End of discussion."

The agenda needs to be open. This allows anyone to add issues that they would like discussed at the meeting. There is one proviso. Anyone adding anything to the agenda must either be at the meeting or assign a contact person to represent them. There is nothing that can waste more time than someone writing an item on the agenda and the initiator of that issue is not present. Invariably, no one will know what that person wanted or means.

It is obvious that the unit meeting can have a significant impact on ownership, communication and problem solving. A negative staff member complains during coffee break about a specific problem on the unit. Others at the table can now respond "Why don't you put that on the agenda for the next unit meeting?" That staff member's response may be "I'm not coming in on my day off just for a meeting." The retort "If you're not going to be there then just ask someone to represent you as your contact person." It gets harder and harder to "bitch." The negative staff are now being forced to take ownership for the problem and communicate it if they want it resolved. In either way the negative staff have been placed in a situation of solving the problem or accepting it by doing nothing. They are now made accountable for their own actions.

3) Setting A Time Limit

The unit meeting or any meeting for that fact needs a time limit - identifying when it will start and when it will end. This time limit must be strictly adhered to - starting on time whether everyone is there or not and ending whether all of the issues on the agenda are completed or not. There is nothing more certain to waste time than an open ended meeting. Any meeting that does not set a completion time or bound by it is ripe for the "run-on-tangent" - talk and talk and talk without being forced to make a decision. A time limit restricts the length of discussion on any one issue, forcing that issue to either be resolved or delayed until the next meeting.

Furthermore, a set time frame allows everyone involved to adjust their own schedule to accommodate the meeting. If the meetings are scheduled for thirty minutes, but the last meeting ran for fifty-five minutes and the one two weeks before ran for forty-five minutes, you will almost certainly hear "I don't have time for this." The maximum time for a unit meeting should be thirty minutes.

When you start and finish on time, you may find that little is done the first few meetings. Once people become familiar with the pattern, most will attempt to get there on time and the discussion will be brief and concise in order to complete the agenda.

4) Assigning A Recorder

This meeting, like any other, requires a recorder. That person's role is to write on the flip chart what is discussed and monitor the time spent on each issue. The unit manager should not be the recorder during a unit meeting for the reasons discussed in the preceding chapter. At the end of the meeting, the recorder is responsible to transpose what is on the flip chart to minutes in a binder.

5) Minutes and Accountability

How many times have you attended a meeting where you heard someone say "What ever happened to 'x'?" Another person responds "I thought you were supposed to take care of that." Another says "Not me! I thought you were." That is all negative staff need to hear. They now have further kindling to light the fire again - "I told you that these meetings were a waste of time. All we do is talk about things, nothing ever happens." Unless we establish accountability in a meeting nothing will happen.

Minutes from a unit meeting must have five headings -

     1) Issues Discussed
     2) Results
     3) Who is Responsible
     4) Next Agenda
     5) Contact Person.

An example is as follows:

Issue	*Results*	*Responsibility*	*Next Agenda*	*Contact Person*
Resident Personal Linen	Possibility of new hampers. To discuss with laundry	John	May 7	Mary

In this way we have not only identified what was discussed, but who will deal with it and when we should receive feedback. The meeting of May 7th would have on its agenda "results of personal linen recommendations." We have created the full communication loop - information in/information out.

6) Using the Results

Let us stay with this example of personal linen. Staff have discussed the loss of resident personal linen at the unit meeting. They made their recommendations to upper management (via the Facility Meeting to be discussed). Those recommendations are then used as the foundation for a new policy on personal linen handling.

What are the chances of that policy being successful in resolving the problems identified?

High! Staff have ownership of the plan. They were involved in its development and as a result will be committed to its implementation. Furthermore, the changes implemented are based on the staff's perceptions, which increases the accuracy of the solution fitting the idiosyncrasies of that unit.

The unit meeting now becomes an active, ongoing problem solving mechanism that allows any manger or staff member to initiate discussion on concerns as they develop. Allowing this degree of unit autonomy ensures that problems are resolved as they occur, conserving the energy, time and resources of the staff and managers. More importantly, this level of involvement gets staff excited

THE FACILITY MEETING

1) Defining The Need

The need for a Facility Meeting depends on the size of the facility. A smaller facility (often less than 60 beds) can combine the Unit Meeting and the Facility Meeting into one. Any facility that has more than one unit may require the addition of a Facility Meeting.

There are some issues that the Unit Meeting cannot resolve. In the example of personal linen, the suggestions brought forward by the staff may involve other units, housekeeping, maintenance, etc. These issues can extend far beyond the limits of the Unit Meeting.

Without any other team problem solving mechanism, these issues must then be channeled from the Unit Meeting to the department head meeting for their consideration. Let us examine the course the information must follow as it passes from one meeting to another and back again.

1) The unit manager relates the information from the unit meeting to the director of resident care.
2) The director of care then passes it to those attending the department head meeting.
3) The department heads are not clear on some of the issues and raise questions that the director of care cannot answer because she was not at the meeting.
4) The director of care then requests information and clarification from the unit manger.
5) The unit manager interprets what was said at the meeting.
6) The director of resident care returns to the next department head meeting and informs those present.
7) The response from the department heads is passed from the director of care to the unit manager.
8) The unit manager then passes this information to the staff at the next meeting.

The whole process resembles a complicated football play waiting for a fumble to happen. The chances of the original discussion being distorted or diluted, skewing the potential solution and that being altered before it is reported back to the initial group is almost guaranteed. This becomes not only an inefficient process, but is ammunition for the "bitching" by the negative staff. As soon as what was discussed is altered because of miscommunication, the negative staff will respond "Why do we waste our time talking about it. That is not what we said. They end up doing what they want anyway."

2) Setting the Criteria

A simple solution is the Facility Meeting. This is scheduled once a month during the first thirty minutes of the department head meeting. At that time, representatives from the Unit Meeting have the opportunity to present issues they could not resolve on their own or recommendations that require the consideration of upper management. In this way, department heads receive first hand information and have the opportunity to clarify what is suggested before discussion is initiated. The material presented then becomes the topic for discussion once the unit representatives leave. Their answer is then forwarded directly to the unit. The full communication loop in a very compact and clear manner.

3) Cashing in on the Results

This process not only allows information to filter from the bottom up (staff to management), but also allows information to pass from the top down (management to staff). A simple example: The administrator receives information that some staff are leaving work early. He doesn't know who they are or the department involved, but is aware that the problem exists and is escalating.

Using the Facility Meeting, he has the opportunity to say to both the department heads and the unit representatives "At your next department and unit meetings, I would like you to discuss the problem of staff leaving early and make recommendations on how it can be resolved." There is probably nothing else he will need to do and still find the problem solved. When the unit representatives share with the staff at the next unit meeting the administrator's request, there will probably be little need for any discussion. Those attending the meeting know very well who is leaving early. The peer pressure created from the meeting may soon stop the practice.

STAFF NEWSLETTER

1) Defining The Need

Two months after the work was completed to develop a new policy on personal linen delivery, you are walking past the dirty utility room on Unit B. You find a staff member sorting resident clothing by the old method. You ask her "Jane, what are you doing?" She responds "Sorting personal linen like we have always done." Your response - "Jane we have spent considerable time and effort both at the Unit Meeting and Facility Meeting level developing a new policy on personal linen. A memo was sent out two months ago outlining it." Her response "*I didn't know about that.*"

Some staff, especially part time, may not know what is happening within the facility if their shifts are few and irregularly scheduled. It becomes difficult for them to keep abreast of all of the changes occurring. On the other hand, the negative staff (the structured, the saboteurs, and those who are dead wood) will use the difficulties in communicating to all staff of a twenty-four hour operation to their advantage. By responding "*I didn't know about that*" to almost anything, they can never be totally held accountable for their actions,

When any staff member can do what they want (through their lack of knowledge or by their devious intentions) regardless of the team's decision, it represents a great deal of power and has the ability to nullify the team's accomplishments.

2) Setting The Criteria

Hence the need for the staff newsletter. A monthly newsletter communicates to all staff the continual operations of a twenty-four hour organization. It is simply a standard sheet of paper, typed both sides, photocopied and a copy attached to *each staff member's cheque* once a month. If certain staff have their cheque pre-banked, then it is added to the cheques that are handed out and the employees must initial that they received the newsletter.

One purpose for the newsletter is to identify policy changes made or memos issued in the past month. On our personal linen example, the newsletter would not repeat what the policy stated, but instead identify the following:

> *New policy issued on personal linen October 14th.*
> *Posted east and west bulletin boards.*
> *To be read by all staff and implemented by October 29th.*

Two months after the memo was issued, you are walking past the dirty utility room and find Jane sorting personal linen. You ask her "Jane, what are you doing?" She responds "I'm sorting personal linen like we always have." Your next response "A memo changing the policy was sent two months ago, didn't you read it?" I would love her to say "I didn't know about that." Your next question would simply be "Did you get your cheque?"

The only response she has available to her forces her to be accountable for her own actions. It is no longer delegating blame "nobody told me" (what she is really saying is "you didn't tell me."), but instead must say "I didn't read the newsletter" or I didn't think that the newsletter (or memo) was important." The next response to either of those statements is:

"In this facility I expect all staff to read the newsletter. The reason for the newsletter is to ensure that all staff know what is happening so that we are consistent in what we are doing. When it is not read, then we only have confusion."

This event is recorded in her Performance Record. If in the next month something else occurs where it is obvious that she has not read the newsletter, specific actions can be taken to deal with her perception and behavior. The staff newsletter is a very valuable mechanism. There is no better way to communicate to a large number of staff who are never all in the building at the same time.

The only alternative used by many facilities is a communication book. Unfortunately these books usually describe a wide variety and multitude of events and issues. Reading them makes it difficult to know what is important and what is not. Furthermore, if a staff member is off for any length of time, it is a horrendous task to try and catch up on the goings on over that period in the communication book. And finally, the only way to ensure that everyone has read the communication book is to have everyone initial it, which is difficult to monitor.

The newsletter can contain a great deal of information. It needs to be brief and concise in highlighting important organizational issues. It can communicate to staff policy changes or memos sent. It can also communicate upcoming changes within the facility.

3) Defining Upcoming Changes

In a work environment that employs crisis intervention, it is not uncommon for the staff to know about a change only after it occurs.

Imagine if this were the case in renovating a unit. (Remember, the priorities of the manager may not be the same for staff.)

Plans are made to move the residents to one end of the unit. A plastic barrier is erected to block off the area that is being renovated. It is easy for the managers to overlook the fact that the dirty utility room door is on the wrong side of the barrier. The dirty utility room may not be a major concern when planning such a massive undertaking as emptying part of a wing. This means that the direct line staff will encounter their problems the day the barrier is erected. The makings of a crisis situation.

The newsletter is a way to overcome this by notifying these events to staff in advance. A standard section of the newsletter is entitled "Upcoming Changes." In the example of renovating the unit, staff are informed in the newsletter two months prior to the scheduled renovation and again one month before -

"The south end of Unit A will be renovated April 7th. A plastic barrier will be erected between rooms 111 and 112. Please address concerns and question to _____ by April 2nd."

This gives staff the opportunity to comment on how this will affect them well before it happens. An effective problem prevention method and an excellent full loop communication mechanism.

4) Keeping Staff Informed

Along with policy changes, new memos and upcoming changes, the newsletter can prepare staff for things like accreditation, government inspections, tour groups, etc. It notifies staff in advance when an assessment survey is scheduled, what is being prepared, who is doing the work, what staff can expect during the survey and who will be conducting it. There is nothing worse than the surveyors or assessors walking around the building, looking in every nook and cranny and no one knows their background, their qualifications to evaluate the facility, their names or even why they are there.

Likewise, the newsletter is useful to notify everyone of the arrival of new staff. It is difficult for many to start a new job. The newsletter shares with staff some basic information about the new employee well before the person arrives - e.g. where he is coming from, how many kids he has, his educational background, the position he is taking, etc. (Of course it is necessary to solicit the permission of the new employee before the information is communicated.) On the first day of the person's arrival, there is an immediate feeling that everybody knows who you are. This creates a secure footing for the new employee and a better opportunity to make that person feel welcome.

The newsletter can also identify staff who are leaving, where they are going and a brief comment on the contributions that person has made to the facility and how they will be remembered. (Again permission must be received from that employee in advance.) A very effective tool to personalize any facility.

5) Caution

Eliminate adding jokes, recipes, etc. to the format of the newsletter. This is a communicational tool. Flowering it in any way will only decrease its importance and value.

The simplest and most convenient way to structure the newsletter is to set a format with pre-established headings - Memos & Policies; Staff Comings & Goings; Upcoming Changes, etc. Whoever is responsible for each area must have their information to the person compiling the newsletter by a certain date - e.g. the department heads must have information on new staff to the secretary by the 25th of the month. The secretary or person responsible for typing the newsletter is only required to fill in the blanks. It is then photocopied and attached to each staff and manager's cheque.

SUGGESTION BOX

If you have or have had a suggestion box, what did it gather? In some facilities usually nothing but dust and garbage. The problem is simple, in order to communicate to the person who made the suggestion, it is necessary for that person to sign it. A staff member who is comfortable enough to sign it would probably approach you directly about the matter. Allowing anonymity provides an opportunity for those staff intimidated by authority to raise a concern or issue.

Remember that you are the "boss." No matter your manner or style, some staff are not comfortable with you only because of your title and position. These staff need an opportunity to remain incognito when expressing their concerns or ideas. That creates a problem for the manager. If you do not know who submitted the suggestion, how do you report back your response? You can spend weeks, even months trying to resolve the problems identified or implement what has been suggested, and that staff member would not be conscious of your efforts.

Not immediately seeing an obvious change to the problem or a solution implemented can be interpreted as a lack of action or even interest on your part. This may not only dampen the enthusiasm and creativity of some staff, it can also provide fertile ground for the negative staff to "bitch" - "I told you nobody reads those things. It's a waste of time putting them in there. They never listen to us."

The solution is again the staff newsletter. All suggestions and your response are identified in the newsletter. In this way you communicate to the person who made the suggestion, and all other staff your philosophy:

> *Come to me directly or use the suggestion box,*
> *either way you will always get an answer.*

A common question about the suggestion box is "How should rude or very negative suggestions be handled?" Put them in the newsletter verbatim. Blank out the four letter words and censor any names, then add below "How do you want me to respond to this?" It demonstrates to staff that you will not withhold comments simply because it is not something you want to hear, and it also demonstrates the challenges you as a manger have in promoting a team atmosphere - there are always those who will abuse what is available to them. By the way, as soon as most staff see the negative comment in the newsletter they know exactly who wrote it.

UPPER MANAGEMENT CONTACT

> *If I looked at the calendar of the upper managers in your facility,*
> *how much time would be allocated directly to staff contact?*

When upper management is not visible within the organization, it sends a negative and critical message to staff that they are not significant. The fact that these managers are probably busy elsewhere is irrelevant, their absence can easily be interpreted as avoidance.

It is important that upper management be regularly visible to their staff. Conducting weekly informal "walk-abouts" for no other reason than to make contact with staff is a common and consistent practice of the effective manager. It is an opportunity to say 'hello' and see how things are going. The scheduling of this contact must be as strictly maintained as the scheduling of any other meeting - difficult if not impossible to cancel, and any cancellation requires re-scheduling in the same week.

In a facility where staff/management relationships are not strong, a more direct strategy in relationship building must be employed. It is valuable for upper management to schedule informal talks with staff. The purpose of these sessions is to:

- reinforce with staff the philosophy of upper management to develop a team atmosphere.
- break the barriers that may have been created by past practices.
- solidify the need for ongoing staff/management contact.
- enhance the staff's perception of their relationship with management and their importance in the organization.
- teach staff how to problem solve and utilize the problem solving mechanisms available within the organization.
- open communication channels.

These meetings provide an opportunity for direct line staff to talk with upper management once or twice a month, i.e. every second Tuesday. These are best arranged over the lunch period. A member of upper management is located in a specific room (a neutral location such as a board room or activity room) between 1130 and 1300 hours. Any staff who would like to join him, to sit and talk are welcome. Staff are encouraged to bring their own lunch, coffee and dessert will be provided. These regular informal discussions or "rap" sessions have specific positive outcomes:

> ⇒   share upcoming trends and projects
> ⇒   enhance staff/management rapport
> ⇒   squelch rumors
> ⇒   identify concerns
> ⇒   teach staff how to effectively problem solve
> ⇒   demonstrate how to use the tools available within the organization (Unit Meeting, Facility Meeting, Suggestion Box, Newsletter, etc.)

These sessions are not intended to break the chain of command. When a specific problem is presented, staff are asked to bring it to their immediate manager's attention and reassured that follow-up by upper management will occur.

Information gained from these meetings can be communicated through the Newsletter and encouraged to be brought to the Unit and/or Facility Meeting. This is an opportunity to deal with issues before they become rumors. Rumors begin by ill-informed or negative staff. It is essential that they are dealt with before they are blown out of proportion. In this way staff are encouraged to take ownership of problems encountered, communicate them to others and utilize the available resources to resolve them.

By the way, few staff may take advantage of this opportunity. When an organization is in need of building trust, it is not as important that time be spent with upper manager, but that staff know and see that they are available. The goal is to avoid being "caught on the spider's web."

CAUGHT ON THE SPIDER'S WEB

We have all seen managers who have created for themselves a spider's web. A complex situation with their staff that has caught them in an entanglement of problems and conflicts. A setting where trust is lacking and it seems that any objective attempts at problem solving are always contaminated. If left on their own, this manager and his staff will only become entangled more and more within that web. Emotions and personalities seem to become the driving force during every contact.

Aggressive confrontation the only recourse available in every and all interactions. It is obvious that few of the solutions proposed at this point can be implemented until the web is broken. To initiate honest and open communication requires aggressive action.

The first step must be made by the manager involved. Nothing will change unless that manager takes the action to make the change. As the saying goes, "The ball is in his court." Other than using the union grievance procedure, staff do not have the authority to make needed change. Making change requires from the manager some basic, but difficult initial steps.

1) He must first admit a problem with trust exists.
2) He must decide that the past is over, regardless of what has occurred.
3) He must avoid the desire to identify who is at fault.
4) He must admit that his personal involvement in the situation will impede his ability to successfully resolve it on his own.
5) He must depersonalize any discussions when looking for a solution.
6) He must learn skills to break the old habits that contributed to the problem.

These steps are not easy, but re-building a fractured relationship is likewise not easy. Once these hurtles are made, a meeting or resolution session can be scheduled.

If left on their own at this meeting, the discussion by the parties involved would soon turn into a "bitch session." The staff in such a situation will have difficulty maintaining their objectivity and focus all of their attention on their manager. Their belief will often be that their manager is the sole cause of all of their problems, whether legitimate or not.

The purpose of this meeting or resolution session is to provide an opportunity to break the emotional hold that has consumed the team and return it to a functioning entity. It is impossible for anyone to run such a meeting if they are the one being attacked. What is needed to maintain objectivity and resolution is a neutral chairperson.

The role of the chairperson is to control any emotional outbursts that may develop and encourage the group to express its concerns. In order to accomplish this, the chairperson must establish some very basic ground rules with the group. Those rules are:

1) *Anything can be discussed as long as what is discussed is an "it", not a "you."* This establishes that any problem can be discussed, but any reference to an individual or position will not be allowed. We discussed earlier that using the word "you" only forces a defensive posture and dissolves problem solving.

2) *We agree to disagree, we agree to agree.* Everyone at the meeting has an opinion and everyone's opinion is valued. The expectation is that opinions will be shared. Once the discussion is complete and a course of action is identified, it is expected that everyone will be committed to implementing it.

3) *What is said is held in confidence.* This is an agreement that as long as rules one and two are adhered to, what a participant expresses will not be held against them after the meeting.

4) *There is no authority in the room, except the chairperson.* Titles, positions, job classification are left "outside the door" and play no part in the discussion. The goal of the meeting is to solve problems. The authority of the chairperson is to ensure that these rules are enforced and to monitor the discussion time on any one issue.

When these rules are observed, the possibility for an open and frank problem solving discussion are quite good.

Unfortunately, some managers who have been in the center of these sessions have stated:

"I'M NOT GOING TO GIVE IN."

If the manager views this as a win/lose situation, then he will most assuredly lose. An offensive posture causes a defensive response, initiating the need for retaliation. To prove to staff that they are wrong and he is right sets an emotional tone that detracts from any discussion on how to deal with the issues at hand. Such a situation cannot be rectified unless the emotions involved are isolated from the problem solving process. There is no easy way to resolve emotional conflict unless those things that flare it up are dealt with. The manager must make a decision - either to fight with his staff or to work with them. If he is tired of fighting, then to work with them requires him to establish the direction on how to remove the strains that exist.

AVAILABLE COUNSELING

We have identified a number of managerial and staff types that create significant problems within an organization. Unfortunately there are some whose problems at work stem from personal problems. We are limited in what we can deal with - marital problems, abuse, financial difficulties, offspring in trouble, alcohol or drug problems, etc. These go beyond the scope of most manager's skills. However, when these problems are not addressed, it does not only result in poor performance and probably high sick time, but the potential for the resident to be at risk.

If the saturation point of a staff member's personal and/or professional stress level is reached, then any slight increase may cause a "blow-up" with a resident receiving the repercussions.

When a staff member is pressured beyond his limit, we have the makings for resident abuse.

Many long term care facilities do not have the resources to employ staff counselors. However, they can tap the resources that exist within the community. It is important that managers establish a contact with the local community counseling services (marital, personal, substance abuse, financial, etc.). Representatives of these agencies can provide staff inservice sessions outlining what it is that they do and how they are accessed. Brochures from each agency can be located within the facility and available to staff. At least when a problem is encountered or suspected, staff can be directed to the resources that may assist them to deal with it.

STRATEGIC PLANNING SESSION

The Strategic Planning Session is a brainstorming opportunity to look back at what the organization has accomplished and look forward to where it is going. This involves representatives from all departments and all levels of staff and management. This session is comprised of two parts.

PART ONE: WHAT HAVE WE ACCOMPLISHED?

This is an opportunity to establish a diary or record of accomplishments, no matter how big or how small. This diary becomes very useful.

1) It provides an opportunity for all staff to recognize what they have achieved.

2) It is valuable to attach to an assessment or accreditation survey questionnaire to assist any assessor or surveyor to know about the organization's history, to understand where the energies have been invested and to demonstrate the growth and direction of the facility.

3) It is the "organization at a glance" for any new manager or employee, allowing them to quickly be "up to speed" on the needs and strengths of the facility.

4) It is a great motivator. It breaks the tendency to look at the 5% that has been done poorly and focus on the 95% that has been done well. It is a way to get people excited about the efforts they have invested to date.

5) Once staff and managers see what has been done, they can better evaluate their next step so they can go further.

PART TWO: WHERE TO GO FROM HERE?

The second part of this brainstorming session is to identify where the facility is headed. This form of brainstorming requires tapping the group's creativity without their being influenced by what happened in the past or is happening now. A successful tool that ensures unbiased analysis is the Magic Wand Exercise.

In this exercise, participants are divided into groups of eight. Each group requires a mix of all departments, as well as staff and management representatives. A recorder is assigned for each group. The recorder's job is to write what the group is discussing on a flip chart and to ensure that the group does not get "bogged down" on any one issue. As each flip chart page is filled, it is taped to the wall. The exercise is conducted in the following manner:

1) Participants are told that their organization does not exist.

2) They are then challenged to identify everything that they would like to see in such an organization. Their discussion is to include environment, equipment resources, staffing needs, communication tools, quality of work life issues, etc. They are to be specific in describing what it is they are presenting and how it will be used - e.g. more staff is not sufficient, it is more staff where and for what?

3) They are to forget about money, personality conflicts, staffing restrictions, environmental structure, etc. They have a MAGIC WAND and can do what they want with it.

4) They are to brainstorm without pre-judging any idea. Some of the craziest ideas can lead to some of the most important issues (i.e. a masseuse for staff can lead to someone asking "How do we deal with staff when they are stressed?")

PART THREE: BACK TO REALITY

The next step is to bring the group back to reality. The groups are asked to scan the list on the flip chart sheets and code each idea identified. They must place one of the following numbers next to each item according to the following criteria:

#1   *Things that already exist within the facility that are working well.*
      Things that already exist within the facility that need to be adapted
        or improved.
      Things that they can achieve with little manpower, resources and
        money.
      Things that will take less than a year to complete.

#2   *Things that at this point seem to require a considerable investment*
        in manpower, resources and money.
      Things that will take longer than a year to complete.

#3   *Things at this point seem impossible.*

It is best when the coding to find the items on the sheets that are the "1's", then the "2's", then the "3's," rather than working on each issue and trying to determine which of the numbers apply.

At the end of the exercise, all the "1's" are placed on a separate sheet. The "2's" and "3's" are filed for later reference. The sheet of "1's" identifies those things that can realistically be done by the organization over the next year. Based on how they were coded, these things are already there, need to be only slightly adapted or require little time or resources to implement.

PART FOUR: CREATING A PLAN OF ACTION

The next step is to place the "1's" in order - the easiest first and the hardest last. This list is arranged in a time frame for implementation, identifying what can be done the first three months, then the second and so on. Through this process, the group has created a schedule for the upcoming year. This schedule can be developed into what can be called a Goal Flow Chart.

The Goal Flow Chart is a process of mapping what the facility has planned for the next three, six, nine, twelve and eighteen months. That map can then be posted within the facility for all staff to see. It not only prepares them for the upcoming events, but shows that the organization is progressing forward.

PART FIVE: MAKING CHANGE VISIBLE

A bulletin board needs to be erected to show the flow of events. It must be divided into three sections:

TO BE DONE	*BEING DONE*	*DONE*

The items on the Goal Flow Sheet progress from one section to the next as they are addressed and completed. Initially the first section will be crowded and few things are seen in the last section. As time passes and progression occurs, the last section grows. Staff see their wins. Their excitement level intensifies.

PART SIX: RE-WORKING THE LIST

At the end of the first year, the group is required to meet again. This time they are to refer back to the original sheets developed from the last session that were identified as "2's" and "3's." At this point it will be possible for the group to add to the list more ideas. The entire list is coded again. Based on the accomplishments made within the first year, many issues will change in their perception. Some of the previous "2's" will become "1's" and some of the previous "3'"s will become "2's." You have now set your goals for the next year.

This exercise can successfully stimulate some worthwhile creativity appropriate to the resource limits of the organization. The end result is a progressive and realistic plan of action.

SUMMARY

Imagine someone constructing a home. When the foundation is built (the most crucial part that must support the entire weight of the building), it is weak and cracked. Little thought is put into the importance of this part of the construction. The person is too anxious to get his home up so everyone can see it. When the home is completed, decorated and landscaped, it looks impressive, but as time passes the weight of the structure cannot be supported by the improperly built foundation. Eventually the foundation weakens and cracks under the load. The house settles and almost every part of it, both the interior and exterior is effected. The walls crack, the floors heave, the trim separates and no matter what cosmetic techniques are employed, the major structural damage cannot be corrected unless sections of the foundation are shored up and strengthened.

Your organization fits this analogy. Your staff are the foundation from which we build all aspects of care. Staff involvement in organizational problem solving dictates the strength of your staff's ability to support what we want to achieve. If the components of effective problem solving (ownership, communication, analysis and resolution) are lacking or poorly developed, it doesn't matter what elaborate programs, policies, decor or facilities we envision and develop, the staff over time cannot cope without the appropriate supports.

Ignoring the problems and forging ahead to develop more and more (the manager who MUST MANAGE) or leaving everything as it is, believing everything is fine (the manager who IS MANAGED) can create so much damage that rebuilding staff's trust and openness becomes a major undertaking.

No matter the role of any staff, their involvement is essential. The guidelines outlining the Unit and Facility Meetings, Staff Newsletter, Upper Management Contact, Counseling Strategies, Strategic Planning Session are just that - guidelines. The challenge on your part is to determine what is needed, what will work and how to implement it. What you need and the extent to which it is employed depends on what you require to strengthen your foundation. No matter what it is you do, it must be in conjunction with the other and critical component of staff morale - what I accomplish is recognized.

Chapter Nine

RECOGNITION

Imagine a married couple with the following dynamics. The husband has difficulty complimenting or showing affection towards his wife. Rarely does his wife hear anything positive about what she is doing, only criticism about what she does not do well or nothing at all. In fact her husband's family life before marrying was one that centered only on criticism. He has not learned how to provide positive recognition of any kind.

On the other hand, his wife prior to her marriage continually heard very positive feedback from her family about her abilities and personal qualities. She learned to enjoy such interactions and as a result of her exposure to positive recognition, she can and does express them freely.

Problems can result in any relationship where one partner is unable to give and/or receive recognition. In marriage, a simple event such as supper can initiate significant conflict. The wife cooks an exquisite supper with all the trimmings, spending considerable time making everything just right. The husband sits at the table and gobbles down the food without a word. When he is finished, he only says "Can't complain about that meal" and proceeds to the living room to read the paper.

There is no question that his wife would feel dejected. Her lifestyle pattern set an expectation that her husband would praise her for the work she did, telling her what he liked about it, how pleasant it was, how much he enjoyed it. She hears nothing of that. Conversely, for the husband his comment was difficult to say and considering his pattern of saying nothing, it had associated with it a great deal of meaning. In a crude and very limiting way he expressed more in those few words than he has ever done in the past. There is no question that over time these dynamics could effect the quality of the relationship.

In order to resolve this potential marital problem, the husband needs to learn a new skill - how to provide recognition to his wife - and the wife must learn to accept the significance of what she does receive from him.

BREAKING HABITS

It is remarkable how many staff in different facilities have commented - "Rarely do I hear when I do anything well, but I can be guaranteed to hear when I screw up." The question that arises is:

In health care, where our mandate is caring for people, why is it so difficult to show that we care for our staff and each other?

This is not a "wishy-washy, sounds nice, but we haven't the time for such things" issue. Recognition is the strongest motivator that can be employed in any workplace. Money is a fleeting and inaccurate measure of accomplishments. Everyone in our setting gets paid the same regardless of the amount or quality of the work they do. There is no piecework, no monetary rewards for a positive quality assurance report, no profit sharing. The revenues generated in our industry are not geared around quality, but are calculated by the number of resident care hours.

Recognition is something that is felt. To demonstrate this, imagine the director of resident care walking down the hall as she arrives to work in the morning. Her eyes are focused straight ahead, her mind on the scores of issues that await her. As she walks past a staff member, that staff member says 'hello.' The director of care doesn't answer. This interaction, or lack of it, is a "felt" experience. It leads to an easy assumption on the part of the staff member - "I'm not good enough for her to say hello?" An obvious example, but a simple one to demonstrate the impact and need for the most basic of recognition.

I often challenge the management team of some facilities "I want you to go onto the floor and find your staff doing something right." It seems so ludicrous that these instructions need to be given to some managers. Some have no difficulty with this task and provide recognition frequently. Those are the managers who usually have the strongest rapport with staff. Others are uncomfortable in providing recognition and find it foreign, attempting to find every possible reason why it is not needed and not important.

The challenges are simple:

- some people expect to receive positive recognition
  frequently.
- others expect to receive it infrequently and do not know how
  to handle it when it exceeds their limit.
- others do not expect to receive it, becoming uncomfortable
  and distrusting when it occurs.

The challenge for the manager is to be comfortable with recognition, sensitive when it is needed and cognizant of those who are not used to it.

CHANGING FOCUS - THE NEED TO SHOW CARING

Withholding recognition has been justified by some managers. Unfortunately, they believe that:

- if you keep telling staff they are good, they will stop striving
  to do better.
- if staff receive a "reward" they will always expect one.
- they are getting paid to be there that is enough of a reward.

You have heard many more rationalizations. In actual fact one of the major things that limits recognition in the workplace is the lack of skills in providing it. Lack of skills is related to a number of factors.

We give what we like to receive.

We are generally more conscious and spontaneous in giving recognition in a way that we ourselves would like to receive it. If I like hearing someone tell me I am doing a good job, I am more likely to provide recognition verbally rather than in writing to those around me. If

I am self-conscious when someone says something positive about my performance in front of others, then I will always provide recognition to others in a discreet manner. Few of us would consider providing recognition in a manner that has no value to us personally. If I think that a letter telling me how well I have performed is too impersonal and cold, I would not send a letter to someone I wanted to compliment. Remember the adage - "different strokes for different folks."

Managers who believe providing gifts is buying their staff and is therefore not needed, miss the opportunity to provide meaningful recognition to a portion of their staff. There are those in our employ who believe - the only good recognition is one you can see. Tell that person "You have done a good job" and it will not have the value a letter of thanks can communicate. In fact some may discount what you say by responding "words are cheap." Give that same staff member a small gift - a meal, flowers, card, etc. - and for him it may hit home. This is a person who needs to hold onto the physical reward that reaffirms his accomplishment.

The value a person places on recognition is determined by many factors - his own life pattern, what he has been taught, what he is used to, his culture, his experiences, etc. Unless an organization provides a variety of ways to show recognition and managers are conscious of the individual needs of all staff, there could be some who are starving in a sea of plenty.

> **We set the value by personal experience.**

The previous atmosphere within an organization dictates the value staff place on the recognition provided. A management team attempting to break the barriers of mistrust by introducing a structured recognition system within their facility, may find their initial efforts unsuccessful. Unfortunately, the frustrations those managers encounter in their initial attempts to provide recognition often results in their judging it of little value and abandoning the venture completely.

A workplace experiencing poor staff morale must overcome the suspiciousness of their employees before achieving the desired results from any recognition system.

In a strained relationship, staff have been conditioned to mistrust the efforts of management.

On hearing or receiving something positive in a setting that for years has been void of such support causes some employees to look for the hidden meaning. The common responses are:

> "What do they want?"
> "They have never done anything like that before. They must be trying to cover up something."
> "Oh oh, here comes the sugar before the pill. There is bad news coming."

Remember, once the seed of distrust is sewn, it takes some time to uproot it.

We decide value based on its accessibility.

Some facilities only have two ways to provide recognition - either everyone gets it despite their performance and/or only those staff who excel receive it. Unfortunately, anything everyone can get can be considered of little value; and things only the best can get are discounted by those who get nothing.

The difficulty when only a few sources of recognition exist is that they may be accessible to only a small number of staff. The average or below average staff may believe they cannot get such rewards, creating a "sour grapes" scenario - "If I can't get them, then they aren't worth anything, so who would want them anyway?"

It is interesting to watch positive staff when they receive the recognition that is rarely available to others. The positive staff almost hide or apologize for receiving it. To some it becomes an embarrassment or something they are forced to discount because it makes them stand out from the rest and can easily create a state of jealousy. Their desire to still be an accepted member of the team may force them to deflect the recognition provided.

The skill of a successful recognition system is its ability to respond to the individuality of all staff in identifying their strengths and contributions to the organization and resident care. The more varied the forms of recognition, the better chance that all staff will receive the positive feedback they need. In this way not all will get everything, but all will get something.

| We do what we are taught to do. |

Providing recognition is a skill. Not all managers are as proficient in that skill as others may be. This requires those managers, as well as staff, to learn how to provide recognition. When recognizing someone for their contributions or accomplishments is ingrained within a relationship, it becomes a natural phenomenon, that is performed with ease and spontaneity.

RECOGNITION ASSURANCE COORDINATOR

Most facilities have someone assigned to the position of "Quality Assurance Coordinator." There is a need to take this one step further. Assign a manager within the facility to be a "Recognition Assurance Coordinator."

We have identified repeatedly that each of us have different strengths and abilities. Some managers find providing recognition difficult. One reason may be that they do not know how to do it, and the other is they are not adept in identifying the opportunities when it is needed. Other managers are highly skilled in this ability. They have a variety of ways to communicate to their staff that they are appreciated and never seem to miss an opportunity to do so. Each facility needs to identify the manager who has the greatest skill in this area and assign that person the role of Recognition Assurance Coordinator. The function of this role is to monitor recognition within the facility to ensure that opportunities are not missed.

Once the opportunity to provide recognition is lost, it cannot be easily regained. When staff expect positive feedback, it is not easy to explain why the opportunity was missed. The Recognition Assurance Coordinator ensures that legitimate opportunities to provide recognition are not lost and at the same time, is indirectly teaching other managers this skill.

When the unit experiences three resident deaths and the staff have dealt with them well, it is the Recognition Assurance Coordinator's responsibility to question the manager of that unit on what she did to show the staff she appreciated their performance. When it is discovered that a staff member has developed a close relationship with three residents, doing extra things to enhance their quality of life, it is the Coordinator's responsibility to question whether that employee's manager commented on her performance and recorded it on her Performance Record. If the staff arrange a special activity for the residents on the unit, this manager would approach upper management to ensure something was done to thank the staff.

By identifying situations where a manager can provide recognition, this manager teaches other managers that same perceptual ability. As opportunities are identified by this manager, they become more visible to other managers. Furthermore, all managers learn from the Recognition Assurance Coordinator what to say and what to do in those situations, assisting them to develop their skills further.

Initially the Recognition Assurance Coordinator's role may be a bit overwhelming. In a work environment where recognition is lacking, she may frequently have to remind others to provide recognition and show them ways to achieve it. Within a short period, managers need only see this manager approach them and their immediate response will be - "Who didn't I recognize for what this time?" This manager now becomes a constant reminder to make recognition a conscious part of the job of managing.

CARE CONFERENCE AND REPORT

We work hard at developing care plans. Unfortunately as caregivers, when it is time to evaluate our efforts, the first thing said is:

"Item number three has not worked. We are still having problems with the resident in that area."

What happened to the other four items identified on the plan that were effective? In order to be cognizant of our accomplishments, we need to create a constant awareness of our successes. It is essential that the team look at what it has done well, along with what it needs to improve. This perception can be achieved by implementing an effective evaluation rule during care conferences and meetings. That rule is - "Before anyone identifies what hasn't worked, they are required to say what has." In this way the team reinforces for itself that its work is not in vain, but very successful in resolving some very complex problems. This stimulates the energy to become more creative for those things that challenge us even further.

Shift report demonstrates the same pattern. What is often the content of the report?

What the previous shift *did not do.*

Listening to report, one can easily question what the previous shift did with their time. The basic rule of evaluation must apply to every report - "Identify first what the previous shift accomplished, then present what it did not complete." In this way it gives all staff insight into the accomplishments of the previous shift and an understanding of why those things were left undone.

Initially these tactics will seem foreign and insincere. In actual fact they are tools that will teach the team a needed skill - how to recognize its own accomplishments. Once developed it will become second nature and be a common occurrence.

Initial recognition

When do staff receive a gift from their employer?

Usually when they leave. It is surprising how many have said "If I would have received the gift before I left I never would have left. Now they tell me they appreciate what I have done."

Imagine a new employee who has just completed her orientation period. She starts her first shift on afternoons with Jane, the most negative staff member in the building. What does this new employee hear from Jane in that first hour? Everything about the place that is negative - "This place stinks. They don't care about us. Watch out for her, she can be one hell of a boss," and so on. In that short time, Jane has the opportunity to tell this new employee everything that she believes is a problem within the organization. Without anything to contradict what she is hearing, this new staff member will probably have her guard up. She will invariably look for something that gives credibility to what was heard. Unfortunately, if she looks hard enough, there is a chance she could misinterpret something that will give credence to the perception of the negative staff. Once it is discovered, this new employee may feel indebted to the most negative employee in the organization "Thanks for letting me know. I *may* have gotten myself into trouble if you didn't warn me in advance."

The following is a simple solution to prevent these dynamics from occurring. The same beginning scenario is in place. A new staff member has completed her orientation period. Her first assigned shift is with Jane. Before the new employee begins that shift, the administrator or director of resident care approaches her and says "We had to hire someone for this job, but of all the people who applied, we hired you. This is a small welcoming gift. We appreciate your joining us and want you to know that you are an important member of our team." The new employee is then handed a gift - a mug with the employee's name or a funny saying on it. The new employee begins her shift and within the first hour hears from Jane "This place stinks. They don't care about us." Those statements create confusion. The new employee is hearing on the one side that the organization doesn't care and in her hand she is holding a gift. How can a place that does not care for its staff still give you a gift for starting with them?

Encountering such a contradiction forces this new employee to be a bit more open minded to see which one is accurate. If the only thing this facility offers is a gift when you start and the rest of the work environment is as Jane describes, then the new employee will soon know that this staff member's perception is accurate. On the other hand, if she experiences a number of things that only reinforces the initial actions of management, then she will see Jane for what she really is - negative. From that point on, her association with Jane is guarded. This simple action strips negative staff of their power.

By the way, if you decide to implement such a process or anything similar, remember one thing - before you start with new employees, you had better ensure that every existing staff member receives a mug first. You can just hear it "I've worked here for fourteen years. I never received a damn mug."

FINDING A GOOD THING

The following are some options for providing recognition and building positive organizational relationships.

1) Recognition for Outstanding Contributions
If doing more than what is required does not bring with it some reward, then why do it? Being recognized as an individual who makes certain contributions is a strong motivator.

a) *Letter of Recognition* - a staff member performing above the call of duty (i.e. establishing a special relationship with certain residents) can find receiving a letter of gratitude from the resident's council very rewarding.

b) *Pins for Years of Service* - is standard in many organizations. Thanking staff for their contributions over the years.

c) *Special Event Days* - an opportunity to provide staff an extra lift on special days - a Christmas party for all staff; free meals with all the trimmings for staff working Christmas and Easter, with the night staff receiving a food tray on those days; staff receiving a carnation on Valentines day; all staff encouraged to wear costumes at Halloween (managers included), etc.

d) *Staff Birthday* - we recognize the resident's birthday, why not the staff's. Maintaining a list of staff's birthdays for each month, and assigning a volunteer to complete a birthday card and attach it to that staff member's cheque can very much personalize the work environment.

e) *A Staff Unbirthday* - these are spontaneous event that just say "thank you." An outdoor BBQ for staff during the summer, where upper management cooks hot dogs, and provides ice cream and lemonade for all staff working that day goes a long way on the recognition continuum.

f) *Staff Appreciation Days* - assigning a regular day to each department once a year - March 3rd is housekeeper's day, May 15th is nurse's day, June 7th maintenance day, September 23rd manager's day. On that day each member of that department receives a carnation or a special lunch. When the staff of that department are encountered on the units, others are to tell them how they contribute to resident care and the success of their job. Having one department responsible for the other department's appreciation day makes it even more successful. When nursing is responsible for this year's housekeeping appreciation day, it is amazing how often a nurse has a camera whenever a housekeeper is in an embarrassing position. During housekeeping appreciation day, posters with these pictures and funny captions are located throughout the facility. Of course housekeeping has to "out do" nursing when it is their turn to organize their appreciation day.

2) Making It Enjoyable

Having fun on the job is a valuable way of creating excitement. There are a number of strategies that can be employed that make the workplace enjoyable. One is the wish list. This is a voluntary event, requiring those who participate to identify *three things they always wanted.* They are to place those wishes in a bowl. Of course, anyone who places their wish list in the bowl, must draw someone else's and satisfy at least one of their wishes. The creativity and levity this creates is impressive. In one facility, a staff member wanted an expensive sports car. He was given a toy replica of a Porsche. Another staff member wanted a husband. A group of staff arranged a series of blind dates.

The secret buddy is another option for relationship building. A staff member draws a name from those wishing to participate. Throughout the year that person is responsible to provide small gifts or cards to the other on their birthday, on valentines day, etc. The secret buddy is also responsible to identify accomplishments and strengths of their "buddy," write them an anonymous note and send it to their buddy with a copy to their buddy's manager. The objective of the secret buddy is to remain anonymous.

3) Blowing Your Horn

These strategies are intended to inform the community that "Our people are good."

a) *Marketing Your Staff's Strengths* - There is nothing more valuable than developing a brochure that professes the specific skills and talents of staff - i.e. the success of the Alzheimer's unit or services, the palliative care program, etc. That brochure should be located in every community building, doctor's office, the library, senior's centers, etc.

b) *Bulletin Board* - Letters or newspaper clippings that praise the efforts of the staff must be posted where they are visible to all. Family or community members who verbally praise the staff should always be encouraged to jot their comments down in a note and then post it as well.

c) *News Releases* - The local paper should be provided regular articles of what staff are accomplishing within the facility.

SOCIAL ACTIVITIES

Many organizations have tried social activities - bowling leagues, baseball games, golf tournaments, etc. When only a small number of staff join, they were canceled. The decision to discontinue a social activity based on the numbers attending makes no sense.

Measuring the success of a recreational program by the number of residents who attend is hopefully long gone. A recreational program is continued knowing that those attending find it enjoyable. The same must apply to social events for staff. Those who attend enjoy it. It enhances their quality of work life. It keeps them excited. When an event is discontinued because a certain percentage of staff did not attend, it has a negative effect on those wishing to participate.

A bit of creativity can make social events successful regardless of the number of staff attending. Creating a bowling tournament between the nursing home, hospital and health unit within the community not only ensures sufficient numbers to allow it to run, but also adds some spice to the event.

If the amount, frequency and intensity of recognition within the organization is low, then motivation is low. When motivation is low, so is quality performance. The more a manager can take an eclectic role in providing recognition to his staff, the more successful he will be in getting all that is possible from his staff.

STAFF EDUCATION

Staff education not only enhances skills, but also excites staff to perform their job more effectively. It is a strong motivator. Yet many facilities have little or no budget for staff training.

If a factory had a change in its product line that required new skills from its employees, imagine the impact on the quality of production if those employees were not trained to adapt to the change. Long term care has experienced a definite change in its product line - the mechanisms for performing care. Yet many facilities have invested little energies in keeping their staff abreast of those changes and needed skills. Without trained staff we can experience nothing but major problems, not only in resident care but staff morale. One philosophy that effective organizations and effective managers hold strongly is - staff education is the key to quality care.

COMMUNICATING INSERVICE SESSIONS

Jane, one of your staff walks by you. You stop her and say "Jane why weren't you at the inservice session last Monday. It was great." Her response:

"I DIDN'T KNOW ABOUT THAT."

In some instances some part time staff may not know about the inservice sessions scheduled. The negative staff on the other hand will use the communication weaknesses of the organization to their advantage. We have returned to the newsletter.

Upcoming inservice sessions are identified each month in the newsletter. The times, topic, who should attend, and location are recorded for each session. The next time Jane is asked why she did not attend an inservice session, she cannot respond "I didn't know about that." She knows the reply to that comment - "Did you get your cheque?" The only response she can make to your inquiry results in personalizing her actions "I didn't think it was important" or "I didn't read the newsletter." Either way we can discuss the issue and record it on her Performance Record. During the performance appraisal we can discuss her attendance at inservice with some accuracy.

PROVIDING INCENTIVES

What motivates a staff member to attend inservice?

If the only motivator is for self development, then those who attend don't need the inservice. If an individual has the personal desire for self development, then he would probably find other ways to learn if the organization did not offer it. The problem with inservice is always the

214

same - those who need it the least will always attend, and those who need it the most will never show up.

The way to motivate staff to attend inservice is to provide an incentive. The following are ways to encourage staff to participate regardless of the shift they work.

1) Certificate of Completion

Many in long term care have received their training through in-house programs or one day seminars. In most cases, these programs compare in caliber to college programs. Providing a *certificate of completion* for the hours of inservice attendance is an ideal way to recognize the quality of the programs and the significance of participating.

This certificate does not only demonstrate a staff member's commitment for self improvement, but can also be of value when applying for another position or job. Imagine the response by a new employer when included with the applicant's letter of reference, is a Certificate indicating - hours of staff training provided yearly is 150, this employee has attended 100 hour. What does that demonstrate about the applicant?

A certificate of attendance can also be a valuable record for any staff wishing to pursue a formal college program as well. Many of these programs have an elective component that recognizes related educational pursuits. A certificate of attendance in many cases may qualify the employee to meet the criteria for that elective, saving time and expense of completing a certain portion of the curriculum.

2) Time in Lieu of

Another incentive to reward staff for attending inservice is to provide time in lieu of hours attended - i. e. when an employee accumulates 24 hours of inservice on their own time, that employee then receives a day off with pay.

3) The Lottery

Some facilities have created a lottery. If inservice is attended on facility time (when you are working) you receive one ticket to the lottery; if attended on your own time, you receive four tickets. The prize can be an all expense paid weekend for two at a resort or a color TV, (a value of anywhere from $300 to $500). The only people who can participate in the draw are those who attend inservice. In either case, an inexpensive investment in staff training.

4) Monetary Incentives

To encourage staff to attend educational programs outside the facility, whether one day seminars or college or university programs, the best incentive is to offer to pay all or half of the registration costs.

In fact the most realistic and appropriate incentive, (one that many facilities are still grappling with) is simple - if you want a staff member to attend any training session you need to pay not only for the registration but their time as well. Learning is part of the job, not a luxury or fringe benefit that is doweled out as though it were a restricted commodity.

5) Inservice Availability

No matter which incentive is employed, staff training has to be more than a forty minute session per week. There needs to be a variety of educational opportunities available at different times and during different shifts. Few facilities have the people power to invest in such an intense training program, but with some creativity, it can be achieved.

a) *Video or audio tape all inservice presentations*. Video cameras now are reasonably priced and a wise investment. The taped sessions can then be scheduled for repeat viewing, i.e. twice each shift for the next three days. These repeated sessions must be treated the same as the original session. Any staff member who has not seen the tape is scheduled to view it during the first shift they are working.

b) A *unit manager or department head is required to present a twenty minute inservice session each week.* That session is taped and reviewed by all other shifts. The responsibility for developing and presenting a session can be rotated through all department heads and unit managers, resulting in each presenting one session every three months depending on the size of the facility.

c) *Renting, purchasing or shared purchasing of video or audio tape training sessions.* Those facilities with a minimal education budget can pool their educational money with other facilities or agencies within the community. This shares the cost and ownership of the programs and dramatically expands their media library.

d) *Organizing seminars with other facilities and agencies within the community.* These are often one day sessions training presented by specialists within the field. Each organization sends an agreed upon number of representatives and all share the costs of hosting the presentation.

e) *Returning what is learned back to the organization.* Attending seminars paid for by the organization must have one condition - those who attend must present a short summary of what was learned to other staff within the facility. That summary is taped and repeated during all shifts.

f) *Providing an up-to-date and accessible staff library.* Staff are recruited to read specific texts and provide a synopsis of what they have read or present a brief inservice session on what they have learned. Their participation in this program gains credits for inservice attendance.

SUMMARY

In this business a strong internal motivation to do the job well is not enough to always spur us to be the best we can be. We all require strong external motivation in order to maintain the drive and incentive to continually give our best. The effective manager is one who knows how to employ such motivating techniques to encourage each of her staff to continue to strive forward. She knows how to excite her staff.

Chapter Ten

THE FINAL CURTAIN

When sitting through a play, we don't leave until it is over. This allows some continuity. We can link what we saw during the first few moments of act one with what happens in the last moments of the final act. The problem with reading any book, is that few of us have the opportunity to read it from cover to cover non-stop. The most common pattern is to read a bit, put it down, read a bit, put it down, etc. until it is completed. Such a fragmented approach results in some of the information presented in the early chapters being diluted, not providing the full thrust of the plot and characters.

What is important for you to do now is to skim through the pages again. Reread each of the headings and sub-headings in each chapter. As you scan the pages, you will find it easy to recall what was discussed and remember the imagery and personal experiences it created for you. It is only in this way that the following exercises can be beneficial.

Start with page one and quickly scan through until you reach this point again.

WHERE DO I GO FROM HERE?

Now that you have reviewed the book, we can take that information and provide some direction on where you go from here. Answer the following questions.

Note: I will not attempt to expand on any of the issues discussed. They have all been detailed in the previous chapters. If you cannot remember what the concept or terminology means, then that is an indicator that you need to review that topic.

1) Where are you on the management continuum?

IS MANAGED----EFFECTIVE MANAGER----MUST MANAGE

2) Where is your boss on the management continuum?

IS MANAGED----EFFECTIVE MANAGER----MUST MANAGE

3) Identify the percentage of staff in your organization who you believe are:

___% negative

___% average

___% positive

4) Rate the following problems in priority. "1" represents the most pressing problem in your organization. Number the remaining in descending order of urgency. Leave blank those that do not apply to your organization.

Psychological
___ staff dynamics
___ game playing

Organizational
___ staff supports
___ resources/workload
___ education

Communicational
___ verbal, too much information
___ verbal, too little information
___ hidden

Interpersonal
___ personality conflicts
___ professional conflicts

5) On a scale of one to five, #1 being weak and #5 being strong, rate yourself on the following issues.

1 2 3 4 5   I frequently involve my staff in problem solving.
1 2 3 4 5   I believe my staff see me as approachable and open minded.

1 2 3 4 5   I consistently recognize staff for a job well done.

1 2 3 4 5   I confront staff on poor performance or attitude.

1 2 3 4 5   I am comfortable discussing issues within a group setting.

1 2 3 4 5   I am comfortable dealing with controversial issues.

1 2 3 4 5   I deal well with conflict.

1 2 3 4 5   My staff know what I expect of them.

1 2 3 4 5   I feel there is a trusting relationship between myself and my staff.

6) On a scale of one to five, #1 being weak and #5 being strong, rate your boss on the following areas.

1 2 3 4 5   My boss involves all levels of staff and managers in the problem solving process.

1 2 3 4 5   He is approachable and open minded.

1 2 3 4 5   He consistently recognizes staff and managers for a job well done.

1 2 3 4 5   He confronts staff or managers on poor performance or attitude.

1 2 3 4 5   He has the ability to encourage discussion within a group setting.

1 2 3 4 5   He deals with controversial issues.

1 2 3 4 5   He follows through on issues discussed.

1 2 3 4 5   He deals well with conflict.

1 2 3 4 5   I know exactly what he expects of me.

1 2 3 4 5   I feel there is a trusting relationship between my boss and myself.

7) On a scale of one to five, #1 being low and #5 being high, rate your organization in the following:

1 2 3 4 5   All levels of staff and management and all departments are involved in evaluating the operations of the facility.

1 2 3 4 5   Staff and managers know the roles & duties of most of the staff of other departments.

1 2 3 4 5   There is effective communication between departments.

1 2 3 4 5   There exists a strong cohesiveness between departments.

1 2 3 4 5   The majority of meetings held for any reason encourage openness, are valuable and productive.

1 2 3 4 5   Anyone in the facility is free to discuss any issue that concerns them .

1 2 3 4 5   People who work here feel good about their job.

1 2 3 4 5   Everyone is held accountable for what they do.

1 2 3 4 5   Everyone is encouraged to think and be creative in what they do.

1 2 3 4 5   The goals & philosophy of the organization are not only expressed but followed.

1 2 3 4 5   Staff and managers feel important and respected for what they do.

1 2 3 4 5   Management is consistent, regardless of who is on or which shift it is.

1 2 3 4 5   Our residents experience a good quality of life.

1 2 3 4 5   Our staff and managers experience a good quality of work life.

What is needed?

8) List ten things you believe are needed within your organization. These can include environmental changes, how the organization is run, communicational issues, resources, etc. Prioritize these from one to ten, with #1 representing the most important and #10 the least important.

	Priority		Priority
1.	___	6.	___
2.	___	7.	___
3.	___	8.	___
4.	___	9.	___
5.	___	10.	___

9) List ten things you believe your boss thinks are needed within your organization. Prioritize these from one to ten, with #1 representing the most important and #10 the least important.

	Priority		Priority
1.	___	6.	___
2.	___	7.	___
3.	___	8.	___
4.	___	9.	___
5.	___	10.	___

10) List ten things you believe your staff think are needed within your organization. Prioritize these from one to ten, with #1 representing the most important and #10 the least important.

	Priority		Priority
1.	___	6.	___
2.	___	7.	___
3.	___	8.	___
4.	___	9.	___
5.	___	10.	___

Where do you go from here?

Scan your answers to the above questions. You have not only identified what your facility and yourself may need, but you have also identified some of the perceptual problems that may exist between you, your boss and your staff.

I am now going to give you a magic wand. I want you to take a piece of paper and write down everything that comes that you would like:

⇒ for yourself to enhance your abilities as a manager.

⇒ for yourself to be able to resolve the perceptual conflicts that exist between you and your boss.

⇒ for yourself to be able to resolve the perceptual conflicts that exist between you and your staff.

⇒ for your organization to enhance its organizational effectiveness.

Be creative. Don't set any limits on money, hours, energy or freedoms. Just let yourself go and identify all of the things you would want to happen. Go ahead!

Now code each issue with one of the following:

#1 *Things I can do easily, that can be completed within a year.*

#2 *Things that at this time may be too difficult or will take too long.*

#3 *Things that seem impossible to me*

Once you have completed this, write all of the "1's" on a separate piece of paper. Place them in order, easiest to hardest. You have your plan of action.

HOW DO I SELL WHAT I WANT TO DO?

1) To My Boss and To My Staff

It is not easy to implement change. Your identifying what needs to be done does not ensure that others may be as receptive.

Once you have your plan of action, you now need to convince others that your ideas will work. One way to sell your ideas is on the basis of a trial period. Take one of your ideas, and rather than implementing it in the entire organization all at once, ask that only one unit or group of staff try it for a specific period of time. At the end of that period re-evaluate it with the input from those involved. This trial period accomplishes a number of things.

a) At the end of the trial period, staff and other managers will be able to see the benefits your idea has generated, gaining their commitment when it is implemented throughout the organization.

b) The trial period requires the involvement of a number of staff and managers to develop, implement and evaluate your idea. This results in their having ownership, increasing their motivation to make it work.

c) The trial period allows a "good idea" to be refined to fit the idiosyncrasies of the organization. When it is implemented by the remainder of the facility, the possibility of it being "bug free" is greater, thereby increasing its effectiveness.

2) Selling Yourself

As children, we have all blown bubbles using a detergent solution and a ringed device. We took time and energy to ensure that the ring was filmed with the solution, then we carefully blew through it in an attempt to get the bubble as large as we could. We then let it go and watched it float through the air. It would soon break and we would start all over again. We never accomplished anything that would last, but we felt good blowing bubbles.

Reading a book can be the same. We read something that spurs us to respond "I need to do that." As we read, we create the imagery of the problem and the solution and decide on what to do. Usually what happens is we return to our everyday routine, becoming so caught up with the demands placed on us, that we lose the motivation to change things. All the energy invested to create the solution in our mind just evaporates.

The intention of this book was to not only challenge you and make you feel good about yourself, but to make things happen. *I know that is what you want.* You have a responsibility to yourself to make a personal commitment to take one step closer to being the manager you want. The work you invest in this final chapter will dictate the success you have in achieving your goal.

IT IS YOUR CHOICE

There is no formula or magic trick to becoming an effective manager, only opportunities to learn the options available and to decide how to use them. That leaves you only four choices.

CHOICE #1 - LEAVE IT AS IT IS AND KEEP FIGHTING
One choice is to keep fighting the system. This is based on a belief that it is not your responsibility to change or challenge the organization, but it is up to your boss and those who you work with to take the initiative. That decision places the responsibility to learn new skills and techniques on others and leaves you to pound away until it happens. To a person who has taken this choice, I ask only one question - how long? Fighting the system is like hitting your head against a brick wall - after awhile your head starts to hurt. This choice only results in your paying the toll by either:

Psychologically - becoming cynical about your job and your role.
Physically - exhausted and frequently becoming ill.
Emotionally - finding yourself constantly frustrated.

When this occurs the symptoms created not only effect you at work but usually at home as well. You may say I am tired of fighting, then your next choice is to *change it*.

CHOICE #2 - CHANGE IT
Everyone has the potential to change their situation. We have discussed many options that can enhance that outcome. What you must decide is what needs to be done and how you are going to do it - the thrust of the previous pages. Unfortunately, change in any organization is usually a slower process than we desire. It took a number of years for the organization to develop to where it is and it will take considerable time to change it into what you want it to be. That means that each step forward must be sensitive to the abilities of those around you and well planned. Some have said "I have tried to change it and it isn't working." Then your next choice is to *change yourself*.

225

CHOICE #3 - CHANGE YOURSELF

If the organization is not changing as fast as you require it to and there are things that are present that you neither have the freedom or authority to change, then you may have to change yourself. That requires you to develop specific survival strategies to exist in a chaotic work environment. You may need to learn how to:

⇒ disassociate yourself from the problems you are experiencing.
⇒ find ways to increase your assertiveness ability.
⇒ feel OK saying no.
⇒ compensate for the things you are unable to resolve.
⇒ challenge those who pressure you.
⇒ leave work at work.

Some have said "I don't like leaving things undone. It goes against my principles." Fine. If *you do not want to change,* and *you believe you cannot change the organization,* and *you are tired of fighting the system,* then that leaves only the last choice.

CHOICE #4 - LEAVE

If you are unable to cope with or resolve the problems where you work, then leave. Leaving is not negative. If you have done everything possible to change the situation where you work and it has not progressed to the point where you feel comfortable going to work, then leaving is essential to maintain your professional and personal well being.

I know no other choices.

THE FINAL WORD

In the first chapter we compared this book to a play. Like any play, you were challenged to uncover the hero, the villain and the plot. Our hero in this play is the effective manager. The villain is the incompetent manager. The plot is the impact of the effective manager versus the villain on our organization's ability to achieve quality of life for its residents and quality of work life for its staff.

It is time to decide your role. It is time to get others excited. It is time you became excited again.

Not The End

BIBLIOGRAPHY

Aburdene, Patricia; Naisbitt, John, *Re-inventing the Corporation*,
    Warner Books Edition, 1985

Adams, James L.; *Conceptual Blockbusting*; Addison-Wesley
    Publishing; 1986

Allessandra, Anthony J.; Hunsaker, Philip, *The art of Managing People*,
    Prentice-Hall Inc. 1980

Athos, Anthony G.; Pascale, Richard Tanner, *The Art of Japanese
    Management*, Warner Books Edition 1981.

Bandler, Richard; *Using Your Brain for a Change*, Real People
    Press 1985;

Belasco, James A.; *Teaching The Elephant To Dance*: Empowering
    Change In Your Organization; Crown Publishers; 1990

Bennett, Dudley; *TA and the Manager*, American Management
    Association 1976;

Berne, Md. Eric; *Beyond games and scripts*, Ballantine Books
    Edition 1976;

Berne, Md. Eric; *Games People Play*, Grove Press Inc. 1964;

Berne, Md. Eric; *The Structure and Dynamics of Organizations and
    Groups*, J.B. Lippincott Co. 1963;

Bernstein, Albert J. and Rozen, Sydney Craft; *Dinosaur Brains*: Dealing
    with All Those Impossible People at Work; John Wiley
    and Sons, Inc.; 1989

Bethel, Sheila Murray; *Making A Difference 12 Qualities That Make
    You A Leader*; Berkley Publishing Corp.; 1990

Blanchard, Kenneth H.; Hersey, Paul, *Management of Organizational
    Behavior*, Prentice-Hall Inc. 1972;

Brown, Arnold; Weiner, Edith, *Super Managing*, McGraw-Hill Inc.
    1984;

Carter-Scott, Cherie; *The Coporate Negaholic*: How To Deal
    Successfully With Negative Colleagues, Managers, and
    Corporations; Villard Books; 1991

Cava, Roberta; *Difficult People*; Key Porter Books; 1990

Charell, Ralph; *How To Get The Upper Hand*; Stein and Day Publishers;
    1978

Covey, Stephen R.; *Principle-centered Leadership*; Fireside; 1992

Covey, Stephen R.; *The Seven Habits of Highly Effective People*:
Restoring the Character Ethic; Fireside; 1990

Dairs, Keith; *Human Behavior at Work*, McGraw-Hill Inc. 1977;

DeVille, Dr. Jard; *The Psychology of Leadership*, Farnsworth Publishing
Co. Inc. 1984;

Doyle, Michael; Straus, David, *How To Make Meetings Work, P.B.J.*
Books Inc. 1982;

Emmerling, John; *It Only Takes One*: How to Create the Right Idea and
Make It Happen; Simon & Schuster; 1991

Freeman, Dr. Arthur and DeWolf, Rose; *Woulda, Coulda, Shoulda*:
Overcoming Regrets Mistakes, and Missed
Opportunities; William Morrow; 1989

Garfield, Charles A.; *Peak Performances*; Avon Books, 1987

Goldhaker, Gerald M.; Organizational Communication, Wm. C. Brown
Co. 1974;

Grensing, Lin; *Motivating Today's Workforce*; Self-Counsel Press; 1992

Hersey, Paul and Blanchard, Kenneth H.; *Management of*
Organizational Behavior; Prentice-Hall Inc.; 1972

Holtz, Herman; *The Consultant's Guide to Hidden Profits*: The 101
Most Overlooked Strategies for Increased Earnings and
Growth; John Wiley & Sons, Inc.; 1992

Holtz, Herman; *The Executive's Guide to Winning Presentations*; John
Wiley & Sons, Inc.; 1991

Hull, Raymond; Peter, Dr. Lawrence J., Hull, Raymond; Peter, Dr.
Lawrence J., *The Peter Principle*, William Morrow &
Co. Inc. 1969;

Ivancevich, John M.; Matteson, Michael T., Controlling Work Stress,
Jossey-Bass Publishers 1987;

Jakubowski, Patricia; Lange, Arthur J., *The Assertive Option*, Research
Press Co. 1978;

James, Muriel; *The OK Boss*, Bantam Edition 1977;

Korn, Errol R. and Pratt, George J.; *Hyper-Performance*; John Wiley
and Sons, Inc.; 1987

Kootz, Harold; O'Donnell, Cyril; *Principles of Management*, McGraw &
Hill 1972;

Kriegel, Robert J. and Patler, Louis; *If it ain't broke...Break it!*; Warner Books Inc.; 1992

Laborde, Genie Z.; *Influencing With Integrity*, Syntony Inc. Publishing Co. 1984;

Levering, Robert; *A Great Place To Work*; Avon Books; 1990

Manz, Charles C. and Sims, Henry P., Jr.; *Super-Leadership*; Berkley Books; 1990

Matteson, Michael T. and Ivancevich, John M.; *Controlling Work Stress*; Jossey-Bass Publishers; 1987

McNeil, Art and Clemmer, Jim; *The V.I.P. Strategy*; Key Porter; 1989

Moore, Terence F. and Simendinger, Earl A.; *Managing The Nursing Shortage*: A Guide to Recruitment and Retention; Aspen Publishers; 1989

Naibitt, John and Aburdene, Patricia; *Megatrends*: Ten New Directions Transforming Our Lives; Warner Books; 1982

Naibitt, John and Aburdene, Patricia; *Re-inventing the Corporation*; Warner Books; 1985

Nanus, Burt; *The Leader's Edge*; Contemporary Books Inc.; 1989

Paul, Kevin; *Chairing A Meeting With Confidence*; Self Counsel Press; 1989

Peter, Dr. Lawrence J.; *The Peter Plan*, William Morrow & Co. Inc. 1975;

Peter, Dr. Lawrence J.; *The Peter Prescription*, William Morrow & Co. Inc. 1972

Peters, Tom and Austin, Nancy; *A Passion For Excellence*; Warner Books; 1986

Petri, Herbert L.; Petri, Herbert L.; *Motivation: Theory & Research*, Wadsworth Publishing Co. 1981;

Quick, Thomas l.; *Training Managers so they can Really Manage*: Confessions Of A Frustrated Trainer; Jossey-Bass Publishers; 1991

Reitz, H. Joseph; *Behavior in Organizations*, Richard D. Irwin, Inc. 1981;

Rodgers, Buck; *Getting the Best our of Yourself and Others*, Harper & Row Publishers 1987;

Rogers, Francis G.; *Getting The Best ...out of yourself and others*; Harper & Row, 1987

Russel, Peter and Evans, Roger; _The Creative Manager_: Finding Inner
Vision and Wisdom In Uncertain Times; Jossey-Bass
Publishers; 1992

Selegman, Martin E. P.; _Learned Optimism_; Random House of Canada
Ltd.; 1990

Stevens, Barbara J.; _The Nurse as Executive_, Nursing Resources Inc.
1980;

Stevens, George H.; _The Strategic Health Care Manager_: Mastering
Essential Leadership Skills; Jossey-Bass Publishers:
1991

Waitley, Denis E. and Tucker, Robert B.; _Winning The Innovation
Game_; Flemming H. Revell Company; 1986

Wellins, Richard S., Byham, William C. and Wilson, Jeanne M.;
Empowered Teams: creating self-directed work groups
that improve quality, productivity , and participation;
Jossey-Bass Publishers; 1991

Whyte, William H. Jr.; _The Organization Man_, Doubleday & Co. Inc.
1957;

Wurman, Richard Saul; _Follow The Yellow Brick Road_: Learning to
Give, Take, and Use Instructions; Bantam Books; 1992

Index

accountability, 26, 73, 78, 84, 128, 147, 169
accreditation, 113
accusatory, 127, 129, 137, 140
adequate equipment, 111
advocate
    team, 164, 173
    team assignment, 173
agenda, 178, 180
aggressive response, 91
agree
    to agree, 153
    to disagree, 153
ain't it awful, 21
alcoholic, 79, 156
anticipating, 129
assembly line fashion, 73
assertive
    response, 139
    role, 125
assertiveness
    negative staff, 129
    strategy, 130
assessment, 168
    survey, 187
assigning success, 60
audience, 131, 133
authoritarian management, 104
authority, 48, 59, 127, 136
autocrat manager, 174
autonomy, 177, 182
average staff, 68, 91, 96
avoidance tactics, 85
avoiders, 120

bad days, 153
bath schedule, 69
beeper, 54
belief system, 19, 35, 79
bitch session, 192

bitcher, 129, 131
bitching, 21, 78, 82, 85, 95, 108, 129, , 139, 151, 158, 183
blowing your horn, 212
blow-up, 194
board, 62
board member, 60, 63, 64
bottom line manager, 57
brainstorming sessions, 116
breaking habits, 202
brick wall, 86,
broken record, 130, 139
budgetary issues, 102, 103
bulletin board, 185, 198, 212
burnout, 76

call to action, 127
capital expenditure, 48
care
    conference, 207
    plan, 139, 143, 151
    team, 91, 103, 164
case study, 149
caught on the spider's web, 191
caution, 9
challenge, 120, 122, 125, 127, 129, 134, 140
change, 179, 182, 185, 192, 198
changing
    focus, 203
    vocabulary, 133
chronic
    burnout, 76
    problem, 143
    staff problem, 141
client
    advocate, 163, 167
    centered approach, 162, 163, 174, 176
    objectives, 163
    responsibilities, 167
cliques, 85
clues, 152
code of conduct, 36
comments meant to paralyze, 120, 122

communicating
    in the "I", 138, 139
    inservice sessions, 214
communication, 32, 156, 162, 176, 180, 186, 190, 199
    direct, 44
    hidden, 32
    indirect, 44
    network, 32
    non-verbal, 32
    verbal, 32
communication
    book, 186
    loop, 177
    network, 32
competition for resources, 48
conflict, 42, 44, 48, 56, 64
confrontations, 137
consistency, 49, 84, 86, 163, 164, 169,
    part time assignments, 165
contact person, 178, 179, 180
continuum, 68
control, 41, 54, 62, 121, 128, 150
controlling a meeting, 135
cookbook on how to manage, 151
counseling, 114, 194, 199
certificate of completion, 215
crisis
    creation, 159
    intervention, 143, 150, 156
    management, 157, 160
    situation, 187
crusader, 38
cueing, 136
cultural shock, 47
custodial care, 89, 164

day shift, 165, 170, 174
dead wood, 20, 23, 68, 76, 83, 87, 91
dealing with an "it", 138
define the direction, 126
defining the dynamics, 92
degree of involvement, 49

delegate blame, 58
demotivator, 137
department head meeting, 43, 63
departmental relationships, 48
destructive criticism, 78
determination, 119
dietary department, 41, 49
directional level, 137
director of
    nursing, 101
    resident care, 64, 101, 105
disciplinary level, 138
discipline, 114
    staff, 137
dismissal, 53, 144, 145
dominating power, 131
double booking, 172
downward spiral, 77, 85, 176
dramatist, 34
drive, 118

education, 30
effective
    manager, 15, 39, 51, 57, 61, 90, 95, 104, 108, 117
leader, 53
outcome, 52
risk taker, 53
effects on positive staff, 83
ensuring accountability, 127
entrepreneurs, 108
evaluation, 168
evening shift, 165, 171
excited, 3, 10
excitement, 118
executive director, 62
external manager, 38

facility meeting, 177, 182, 191
fighting the system, 87
finding a good thing, 210
fire starters, 158
follower, 121, 122, 124

four hour or spot shifts, 173
fun in the work place, 154
game playing, 18
get "dirty", 154
getting even, 23
goal flow chart, 116, 198
grievance, 127
group, 121, 132, 135, 150,
   dynamics, 18
   manipulation., 80
   presentation technique, 133
   process, 38
gun shy, 60, 64, 150

hidden,
   agendas, 37
   channel of communication, 60
   communication, 32
horizontal organization, 40
hospitals, 51
housekeeping, 41, 47, 50

"I" assertion, 127
I'm only stupid, 19
ideal organization, 16
imagery, 132, 133, 140
impact
   manager who must manage, 96
   manager who must manage on managers, 98
   manager who must manage on residents, 99
   manager who must manage on staff, 97
   of negative staff, 92
   negative staff on managers, 95
   negative staff on residents, 93
   negative staff on staff, 94
incompetent manager, 37
inconsistent
   assignment, 164
   management, 73, 75
informal discussions, 116, 190
initial recognition, 113, 208
initiators, 120

inquest, 147
inservice availability, 216
interdepartmental
    jealousy, 48
    relations, 41, 47
    relationships, 40
internal manager, 37
intimidates, 132
iron fist in a velvet glove, 56
is managed, 51, 56, 60, 65, 121, 124, 140, 150
islands, 47, 164

kicked, 74
keeping score, 23

lack of skills, 203
lateral reporting process, 49
length of primary team assignment, 173
let's you and him fight, 21, 24
letter of recognition, 210
limitations, 7
lineal authority, 102
lines of
    authority, 48
consistency, 49
lateral reporting process, 49
loa without pay, 114
long term care, 3, 13, 15, 19, 30
lottery, 215

magic wand exercise, 196
maintenance staff, 51
making it enjoyable, 211
manage your manager, 125
management
    assertiveness, 138, 140
    consistency, 150
    contact, 114
    continuum, 61
    dynamics, 6, 62
    success, 61
manager who

is managed, 13, 23, 90, 94, 97, 105, 117, 161
who must manage, 12, 51, 61, 90, 95, 105, 117, 161, 121, 140, 150
managers
    accountability, 146
    confidence, 150
    manual, 143, 149
    power, 2
    role, 106,
marketing, 212
mask of management, 34, 152
master
    rotation schedule, 113, 165
mechanical, 69, 73
meetings, 115
memos, 112, 115
mental imagery, 133
mentally impaired, 31, 70, 71, 81
merry-go-round, 23
minutes, , 64, 135, 178, 183
monetary incentives, 216
money, 69, 77
morale, 12, 14, 19, 23, 29, 33
mosquito annoyances, 29
motivate staff, 109
motivation, 90, 104, 110

negative resident, 124, 129
negative
    staff, 68, 77, 91, 121, 124, 129, 138, 151
    suggestions, 189
new
    resident, 30
    staff, 187
news releases, 212
night shift, 165, 170, 174
non-verbal communication, 32
now I've got you, you SOB, 23
nurse manager, 23, 31
nurse's training, 71
nursing, 101
    department, 41
    supervisor, 101, 104

objectivity, 128
off shifts, 170
organizational chart, 48
outstanding contributions, 112
ownership, 108, 156, 159, 170

part time
    schedule, 165
    staff, 163, 165, 171
participatory
    decision making, 115
    management, 52
passive/aggressor, 74
peak demand, 45
people manager, 11
perception, 119, 125, 129, 133, 142, 149
performance
    appraisal, 115, 141, 144
    standards, 53
permission, 26
persist, 120, 125, 130
personality
    conflict, 35, 142
    make-up, 36
    qualities, 36
personalized resident care, 163
pins for years of service, 210
plan of action, 197
planting the seed, 56
policy change, 185
poor performance, 52
positioning, 134
positive
    feedback, 201, 206
    staff, 68, 87, 90, 96, 108
power, 19, 24, 25, 68, 78, 80, 84, 88, 121, 129,
    struggle, 80, 83
present to a group, 133
priority, 125, 127
problem solving, 44, 47, 52, 63, 123, 138, 143, 150, 156
professional
    conduct, 36

conflicts, 35
providing incentives, 214
pseudo caring, 80
psychological
    dynamics, 17
    games, 18, 24, 129, 139
putting out fires, 150, 156

quality
    assurance coordinator, 206
    care, 3, 5, 30
    of life, 6, 57, 68, 73, 80, 85, 89, 162

rap sessions, 190
recognition, 19, 129, 201, 210, 213
    assurance coordinator, 206
recorder, 135, 150, 181
recreation department, 41, 42
reflex response, 140
replacement shifts, 165
report, 207
reprimand, 53
    dismissal, 53
    verbal warning, 53
    written warning, 53
rescuer, 19, 25, 68, 75, 83, 91
resident
    abuse, 88
    care, 41, 101, 111
    grouping, 164, 166
resist, 120, 124, 128, 148
resolution, 156
resource
    manager, 11
    shortages, 127
risk taking, 107
rules, 193
rumors, 33, 191

saboteur, 21, 24, 68, 73, 83, 91
secret buddy, 212
self

gratification, 76
directing environment, 107
fulfilling prophecy, 78
governed, 163
image, 18, 24
managed, 104, 107
righteous, 85
seniority, 171
setting
a schedule, 178
limits, 87
shifts, 42
short-sighted managers, 6
sick time, 77, 86, 88, 171
significant other, 80
social activities, 113, 212
special event days, 210
staff
appreciation days, 211
assignment, 164
birthday, 211
education, 213
mix, 77
morale, 14, 108
newsletter, 115, 184, 199
of the month, 113
performance record, 141, 151
unbirthday, 211
vacation, 171
staff supports
accountability, 26
permission, 26
staffing dynamics, 17, 68
average staff, 68
negative staff, 68
positive staff, 68
staffing pairs, 164
standards
of nursing practice, 103
of performance, 140, 142, 150
steps in implementing the client centered approach, 174
strategic

planning session, 195, 199
stress, 86, 87
    days, 114
    level, 194
stripping power, 131
structured staff, 68, 69, 70, 71, 72, 77, 83, 91
suggestion box, 115, 177, 188, 191
support
    group, 114
    services, 111
survival technique, 125

taking a stand, 121
talking in the positive, 138
task oriented, 69
team
    approach, 52
    conferences, 111
    configuration, 164
time
    in lieu of, 215
    limit, 180
training, 71
trial and error, 149
trial
    basis, 148
    period, 174
trust, 83, 88, 96, 105, 191, 199
turn-over, 88

unilateral action, 127
union, 135, 147, 158
    grievance, 59
unit
    autonomy, 163
    manager, 65, 101, 105
    meeting, 177, 182, 191
unwritten rules, 69
upcoming changes, 186
upper management contact, 189
upward spiral, 176
verbal communication, 32

    diarrhea, 33
    information overload, 33
    recognition, 113
    rumor, 33
vertical organization, 41
video tape, 216
volunteers, 169

walk-abouts, 190
weak self image, 23
well adjusted response, 91
wheel-barrow, 11, 28
    imagery, 61
wish list, 211
withdrawn response, 91
work
    assignments, 112
    environment, 111
    load, 112, 166, 173
working managers, 104, 105
written
    communication, 126
    recognition, 112
    warning, 53

yes, but, 23